The Young Adult's Manual
to a Successful Life

Interactive Workbook

It's LearnTime!

The Young Adult's Roadmap
to a Successful Life

On the Reelz
PRESS

— by —
FREDERICK & SHARON GOODING

This book is written as a source of entertainment and information only. The suggestions made herein are not to

substitute qualified, professional help.

ISBN: 978-0-9778048-3-2

Printed in the United States of America.

While every precaution has been taken in the preparation of this book, the publisher and authors assume no responsibility

for errors or omissions, or for damages resulting from the use of the information contained herein.

On the Reelz Press books may be purchased for educational, business, or personal use. E-book editions are also available at

www.amazon.com. For more information, contact On the Reelz Press corporate/institutional sales department at http://

otrpressinfo.wixsite.com/website.

Special thanks to Rudy,

and of courserous to one #1 fan . . .

TABLE OF CONTENTS

ROADMAP

**I keep six honest serving-men
(They taught me all I knew);
Their names are What and Why and When
And How and Where and Who.**

*Rudyard Kipling
(The Elephant's Child)*

WELCOME TO IT'S LIFETIME!

Welcome! My name is Sharon! Together, we are THE GOODING TEAM! we make success more systematic Young Adults.

My name is Frederick! Our bottom line is that and less dramatic for

On the previous page, we start with the timely quote from Rudyard Kipling, but we are going to call his six honest serving men our six horsemen -- after all, one cannot drive far without horsepower, true? In this chapter, our six horsemen will help outline what this powerful manual is all about, and give clues about how the reader can unlock its true power and potential.

Hay! This is a picture of a horse, by the way...

WHO

This interactive workbook is designed for Young Adults between the ages of 12 - 24. More specifically, this manual is for the Young Adult who wants to "make it," "have it all," or generally "be successful" in life, but is not 100% sure about how exactly that success will occur. We thereby provide practical pointers about "this thing called life" so that you do not spend most of your time "spinning your wheels" in search of success. This easy-to-follow workbook features five action-packed chapters, which coincidentally, mirrors the typical five gears that a classic stick shift vehicle contains. This means that you are encouraged to go at your own speed. Some sections will take no time at all to complete while others might "throw you for a curve." Take your time either way, it's your life.

- if you are a Young Adult:

This workbook serves as a supplement to the teachings and advice of your parents, relatives, teachers and all the other supportive members of your local community. Although you may have familiarity with many of the concepts contained within this workbook, you will be challenged to think about these ideas in new ways.

- if you are not a Young Adult:

This workbook serves as a "hands on" teaching tool that is both practical and applicable for the Young Adult you have in mind. The exercises and emphasis of creating a Roadmap, or a plan for future success, will particularly benefit student athletes or aspiring performing artists who run the risk of over-esteeming their chances of making it to the "big time" at the expense of their present academic opportunities.

While making mistakes is a part of life, why must Young Adults make the same mistakes that we older adults made when they do not have to? Quite simply, there is no need for Young Adults to "reinvent the wheel."

This manual and all of the exercises contained herein revolve around the Roadmap Rubric which reflects that a planned course of action is strongly recommended in order to maximize one's chances for success in this LifeTime. Why? Whenever you come up with a plan, you have a much better idea about where you are going and what you are doing. Instead of guessing what comes next, you now have direction. Therefore, the more concrete your plan, the more concrete your chances to succeed. Period. While we cannot guarantee one's success by merely creating a plan, we do guarantee that success is more difficult to achieve without one.

Alas, we cannot prevent all Young Adults from making mistakes, since mistakes are a natural part of life. Yet, we can help you prepare for the road ahead by minimizing delays from common detours typically caused by manageable and preventable mistakes. This proactive approach will enable you to travel through life more comfortably positioned in the "driver's seat." Ultimately, this workbook's "success" will be judged by your drive to succeed; meaning, the more fuel that you put into the activities, the more mileage you will get out of the workbook.

We are well aware that success means different things to different people. While we do not know exactly what your definition of success includes, what we do know is that your success is the combination of several goals and accomplishments which will necessarily involve the five major Decision Points. Whether you decide you want to include these five factors into your plan or not, these are major, life-impacting factors that you will have to make a decision about at some point in your life.

Decision Point	"What's the Point?"
1 CAREER	to have a successful, fulfilling and rewarding occupation
2 EDUCATION	to gain respect and admiration for being genuinely qualified and skilled at your craft
3 CAPITAL	to obtain sufficient cash and credit to comfortably finance your desired lifestyle
4 POSSESSIONS	to apply your capital towards the acquisition of objects that will enhance your life experience
5 COMPANIONSHIP	to blissfully share your lifestyle with your dream mate and/or to have smart, healthy and beautiful children that further your legacy

Now, a word about this workbook: Typically when counting, people start with the number one and skip the number zero. Similarly, when it comes to success, many start by talking about their desired results while skipping over the fundamental steps necessary to achieve such results. Thus, before we begin in earnest, we take the time to properly introduce key concepts developed throughout the book. This way, there will be "zero" chance of confusion!

WHEN

Now is the absolutely best time to be using this workbook, of course! If you are a parent, guardian or educator, feel free to use the chart on the following page to help you gauge how to best effectively use this tool for the Young Adult you have in mind. "Awareness" = introductory exposure to concepts, "Prep" = more intensive exploration of concepts.

YOUNG ADULT READINESS CHART

Level →	6th	7th	8th	9th	10th	11th	12th	College Frosh	College & Beyond
College Awareness	√	√	√	√	√	√	√		
College Prep				√	√	√	√		
Career Awareness	√	√	√	√	√	√	√	√	√
Career Prep						√	√	√	√
Life Skills Prep	√	√	√	√	√	√	√	√	√

The above metric is of course recommended and is not absolute. Depending upon your knowledge of the Young Adult, you may determine how best to frame and emphasize the material contained herein. The following skill sets are addressed:

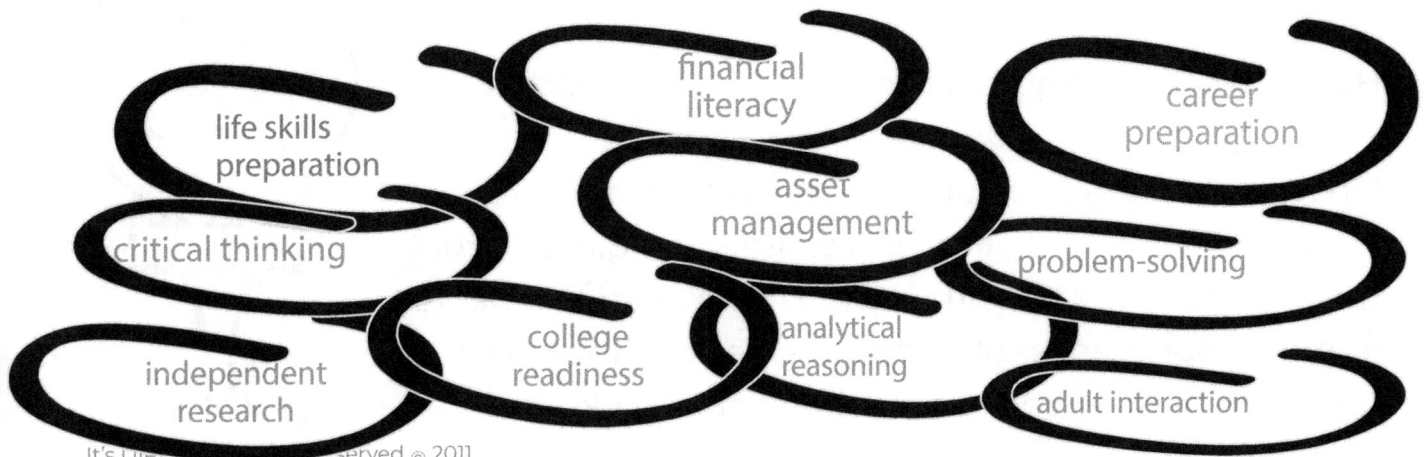

life skills preparation

financial literacy

career preparation

critical thinking

asset management

problem-solving

independent research

college readiness

analytical reasoning

adult interaction

WHERE

This workbook can be completed on your own at home, at school, at church or in a group setting with friends. At times you will be asked to go beyond this workbook's boundaries and conduct a little bit o' research (which we hear does wonders for your cholesterol levels!), which also means that your local public or school library will come in quite handy here. The internet never hurts, but if you do not have access at home, then your local or school library should be of service as well. Not only are we putting the "work" in homework, but also, in the process of having you constantly commit to responses, we underscore the fact that in the road ahead, you will consistently be forced or asked to make decisions -- and live with them -- whether rightly or wrongly.

WHY

So before we go any further, a fair question to ask is "Why go any further?" Most of you reading this probably feel that you have a very good idea of what you wish to do later on in life, which we imagine, incorporates some idea of success rather than failure. But how to do it all and have it all? Does success simply boil down to hard work or hard luck?

Well, take a look at this golf ball:

Have you ever hit a golf ball before? Miniature golf ball?

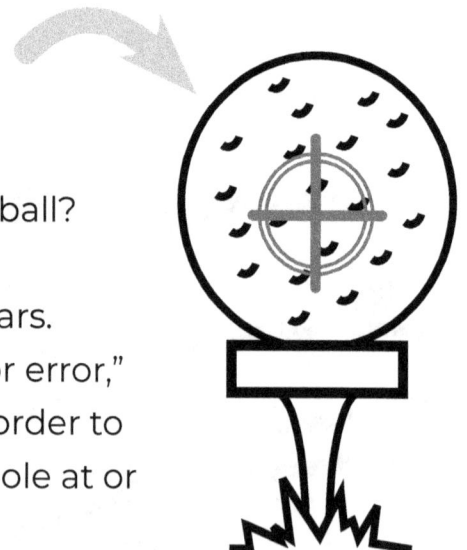

If not, it is actually more difficult than what it appears. Partly, the reason is that there is so little "margin for error," meaning you have to hit the ball EXACTLY right in order to improve your chances of getting the ball into the hole at or under the recommended par, or allowable strokes.

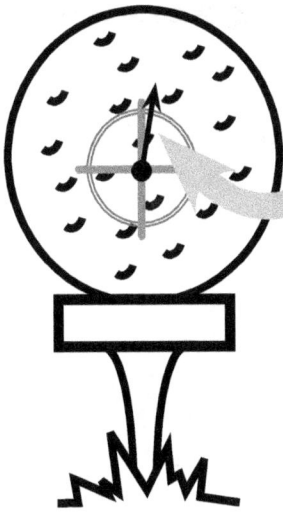

Well, here's where it gets interesting. If you look at the arrow to your left, as you can see it is not really "off the mark" by that much -- it appears to miss a direct hit by only a couple of degrees. No big deal, right? Maybe not over the short term, say, if the ball travels only a few feet. But as you can see from the illustration to your right, not hitting the ball directly on target really starts to make a major difference the further the ball travels, especially when you're talking about hundreds of yards along the fairway, landing you in the "rough" and making it more difficult for you to make it to your desired destination.

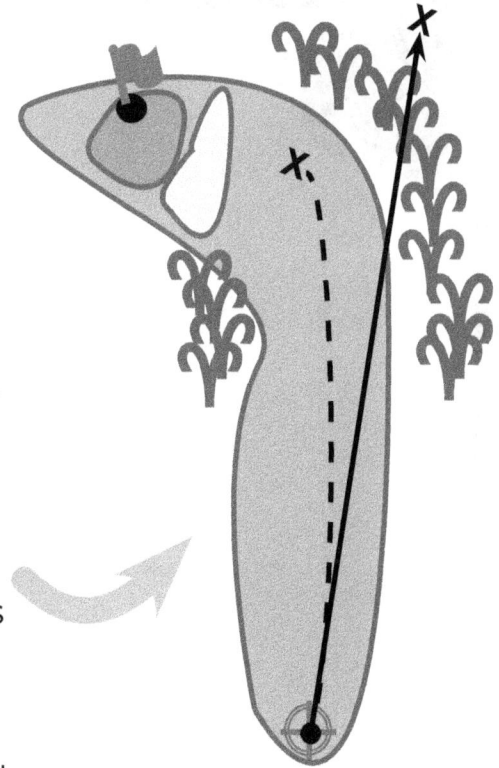

Do you see the magic of this metaphor? The better able you are able to orient your direction early in life, the better off you will be in reaching your destination of success later on down the road. Unlike golf, luckily you do not have to be PERFECT in deciding right now what you want to do with the rest of your life and how you want to do it. But, the closer you are to pin-pointing where you want to go with your Roadmap now, the smoother your ride will be with less backtracking later.

HOW

OK! Now we promised to "change your life," but HOW?

Here is where we get down to the nitty gritty and explain how you can get the "maximum mileage" out of this manual. Turn the page to see what we're saying:

1

PUT ME ON THE MAP ACTIVITY

...map below and label the map in the ...manner.

⭐ = *Capital*   **H** = *homebase*

1 = *top college choice #1*
2 = *top college choice #2*
3 = *top college choice #3*

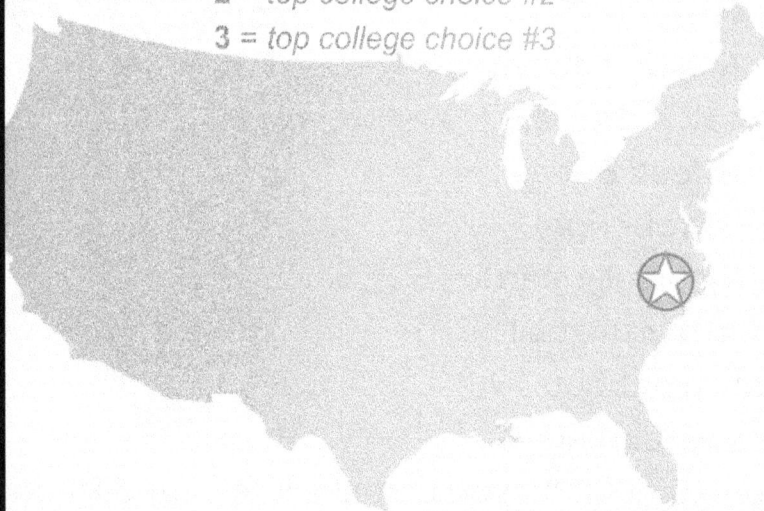

Where specifically are the locations of your top college choices?

Are your top college choices near or within the state where you ultimately wish to live after college? Label where you wish to move as **M**.

Now draw lines from your top college choices to **H**. For your #1 college choice:

The approximate distance in miles: _____

...t will take _____ hours to get home and th... average cost will be $ _____ via _____
(plane/train/bus/car)

...will likely travel home _____ times a semester
...r _____ times a year.

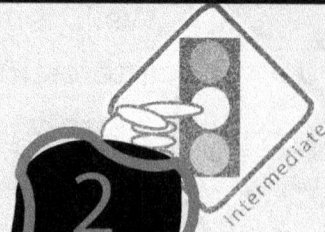

2

Intermediate

Many schools have different tuition rates for different students. For instance, graduate students pay a different fee from undergraduates, students who stay on campus with a meal plan pay a different fee than those who live off campus, etc.

For starters, determine any differences in tuition for in-state vs. out-of-state residents. The rules vary, but typically you are considered an out-of-state resident if you have not established residency for a year prior to beginning the application process.

If this applies to you, how will the difference affect your decision? Will it increase the amount of your school loans? Does it make sense to apply, take a year off and then move? Conversely are there special scholarship opportunities for in-state residents?

4

3

3

Map out a possible route to visit in-state or nearby schools on your list of possibilities. Aside from a formal tour, are there any upcoming events where you can "drop in" to see what the vibe on campus is like?

Advanced

To your left on page 8 is a sample page from the non-stop action that shortly awaits you. Just so you know, there are a couple of special features that we wish to explain. At Point #1, the STANDARD activity takes up the main space of the page. Young Adults using this workbook for "awareness" (see chart, pg. 5) should complete this section. At Point #2 is the INTERMEDIATE activity as denoted by the "yellow" traffic light and builds upon the standard activity. Young Adults using this manual for "prep" may proceed to the ADVANCED activity at the bottom of the page, as illustrated with the "red" traffic light (Point #3)for complete mastery of the concept. The logic of the exercises are practical, but sequential. For best results, we recommend doing all three exercises in order.

Notice at Point #4 a camera with a flash. The camera signifies that on this page, several of the answers asked for in the main space will serve as a "flash point." Just like a treasured photograph, remember this point as you will likely be asked to return to it later in the chapter when you conduct your Rearview Review. The number inside of the camera corresponds with the "scenes to capture" that you are alerted to at the very beginning of the chapter. Other signs to look out for include:

Key Question - every chapter starts with a broad question that helps you frame the material you will experience throughout the chapter.

The Bottom Line - this sign at the conclusion of the chapter is key; the answer you provide here will also serve as the same answer that you plug into your Roadmap.

Brain Storm - there is at least one in every chapter; take advantage of the space provided to get out some very important thoughts.

Connect the Dots - found at the bottom of the Brain Storm page and also at the bottom of the Roadmap page, this activity helps organize the thoughts on the page.

Fuel for Thought - usually found at the end of the chapter, this sign signals good ol' fashioned advice that ties together the whole theme of the chapter.

Word Block - found intermittently throughout, this sign signals a familiar or unfamiliar word that we wish for you to pay special attention.

Rearview Review

Rearview Review - this is where we help you put all the hard work you invested throughout the chapter in one place. By looking back in a constructive manner at the chapter's Flash Points, we arrive at a Decision Point.

Roadmap - this sign means that we have come to the end of the road -- for that particular chapter, that is. Be sure to fill in the Decision Points you reach along the way.

Congratulations!
Now that you have successfully reached this Decision Point, you have unlocked a bonus
SIGN OF THE TIMES

? ? ?

?

Bonus Checkpoint - as a reward for your travels, this feature reveals a bonus sign that will be unlocked for future chapters

By planning ahead, we expect for you to avoid the dreaded Rat Race that so many of us feel we have to run. Plan and run ahead!

Ask Your Folks - get your folks in on all of this fun! Here, you are encouraged to obtain feedback and information from those who have a bit more "mileage" than you do.

Lastly, do not forget Chapter OVERDRIVE located at the end of this manual after Chapter 5 -- you will find it helpful in preserving all of your hard work.

Be ye forewarned: we're not trying to be obtuse by subjecting you to a non-stop barrage of questions, but these are questions that you can handle. We "build up speed" as we cruise through our Decision Points, meaning we do not start off with epistemological questions about the "meaning of life."

We start off with simple questions that you can quickly answer that revolve around things that you are interested in, and lo and behold, once we review the ground we have covered in the Rearview Review, we soon discover that we have the makings of a mastermind plan to be successful and RULE THE WORLD! Mwa ha ha ha! Oops! We're getting a little carried away here -- let's just focus on answering the questions first...

LET'S GO!

We firmly believe that after you complete this workbook, not only will you have a practical, tangible and feasible Roadmap, or plan for your future actions, but you will have a clearer understanding about how to obtain the success that you envision for yourself.

Recall, we cannot guarantee one's success by merely creating a plan. But we do guarantee success is more difficult to find without one. Consider this workbook as your next practical step towards realizing REAL and not just imagined success.

Avoid the dreaded Rat Race!

Pursue the winding road to success instead (in our opinion, it's indisputably more scenic).

Now let's get going! Not only is Chapter 1 impatiently awaiting, but dare we say, your LifeTime! as well...

**Sincerely,
Sharon
&
Frederick**

The Gooding Team

CAREER

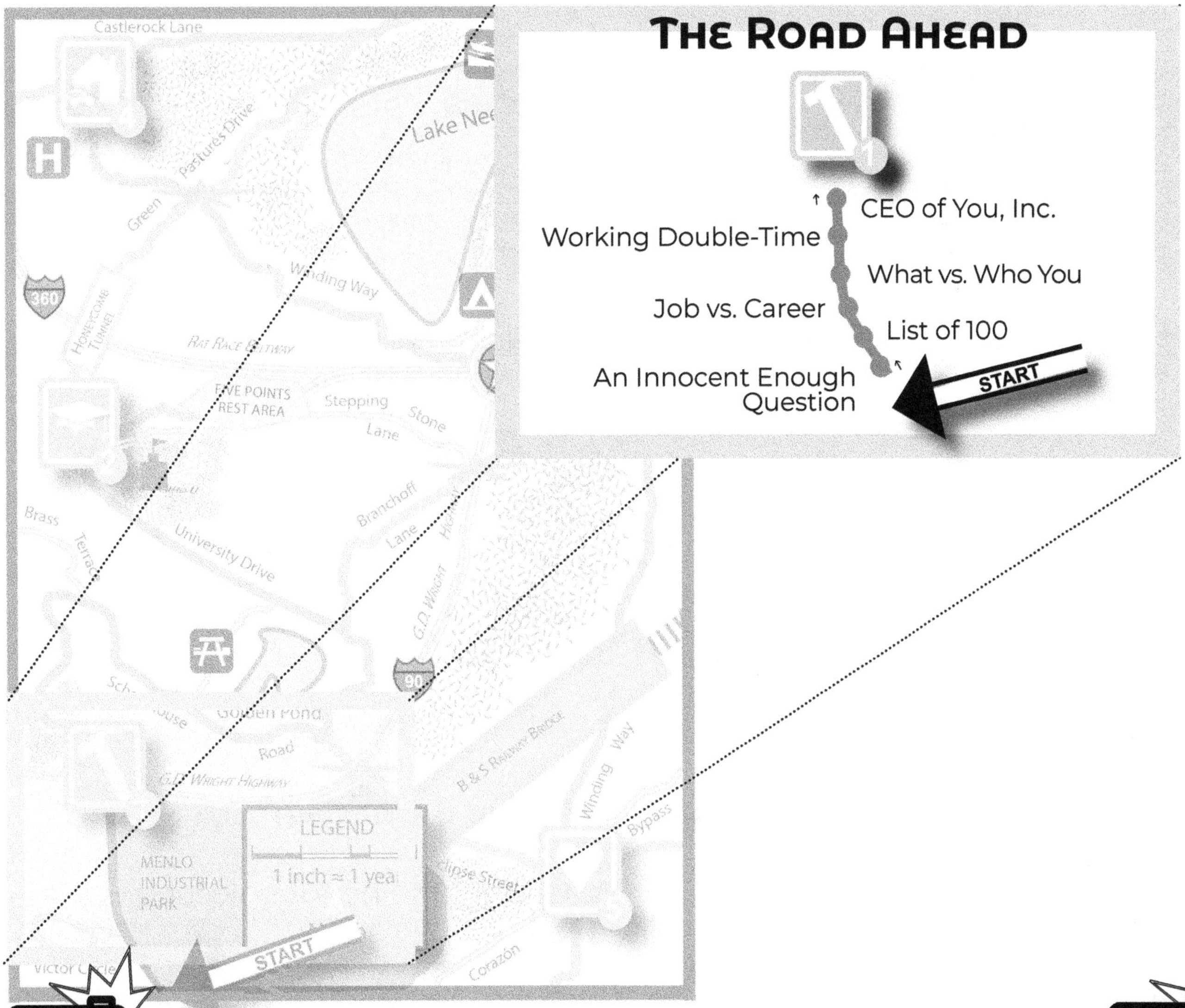

THE ROAD AHEAD

CEO of You, Inc.

Working Double-Time

What vs. Who You

Job vs. Career

List of 100

An Innocent Enough Question

START

Flash Points You Must See in this Chapter

1. A concrete answer to the dreaded question: "What do you want to do when you grow up?"

2. 100 specific career options outside of the doctor/lawyer or sports/ entertainment paradigms.

3. Weather your own Brain Storm and rediscover the things you already enjoy.

4. Learn the difference between finding a job and creating a Career.

5. How to "think twice" when thinking ahead and plan for two Careers.

6. Effective strategies for you to start branding yourself and communicate your worth to others.

List five (5) things that you enjoy and would define yourself as really good at:

1)

2)

3)

4)

5)

Now ask yourself:

"Who is better at what I want to do?" [name at least 3 people]

"Why does the world believe that this person is better?"

"What would it take for me to perform these tasks at an expert level?"

KEY QUESTION

Why would anyone want to use a Roadmap? Are they truly helpful tools or do they only help out a little bit? Have you used one before? When and why?

AN INNOCENT ENOUGH QUESTION

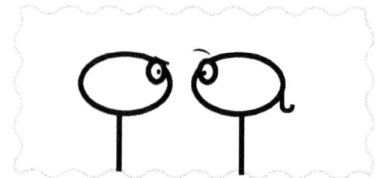

"soOOOOOo, what do you want to do when you grow up?"

A) if you know the answer

What does the handbook suggest?

B) but if you don't know the answer

What does the handbook suggest?

Everybody makes a living selling something, whether it be a product or a service. What will you sell and how will you personally profit?

"Everybody makes a living
selling something"

WAIT! Is the above statement true? Does everybody make a living selling either:

a) a product?

or

b) a service?

If not, list some exceptions to this rule and explain why. C'mon now! Don't be shy:

a

b

c

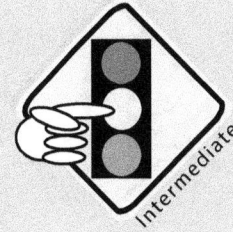

Hey! An expert is merely one who has mastered a particular product or service that they offer to others. Find an expert in one of the five "things" you listed on page 14, whether it be locally or out of state, and "map their training"; meaning, find out as much as you can about what steps they took with respect to Education and training before they became known as an expert in their field.

KEY QUESTION

Why is CAREER the first Decision Point ahead of EDUCATION?

We cannot stress enough that it is best to first figure out what to do, then secondly figure out how to do it. What you want to do will influence greatly what type of education you should pursue. The key here is to avoid the common pitfall of becoming so focused on the goal of "getting into college," that you forget or do not take time to remember why you are "going to college" in the first place!

After "mapping the life" of the expert you chose, contact them, inform them you are conducting research for an educational project and interview them to discuss their personal experiences. Take notes!

Intermediate

While we're on the topic of high-paying jobs, a key question is where do you need to go to make an above-average living?

For the ten positions that you listed in the column to your right, are any specific to a particular geography or region in the country?

Are all of these positions universal, or are some specific to metropolitan living while others are unique to the suburban or rural environments?

Think of ten jobs that represent the highest-paying professions that you know. Next to the listed profession, list what you believe the average annual salary to be.

LIST OF HIGHEST-PAYING PROFESSIONS

Profession	Salary
1)	
2)	
3)	
4)	
5)	
6)	
7)	
8)	
9)	
10)	

Advanced

Look closely at the list and determine what are some of the desirable personality traits commonly associated with the professions you listed. If you find similarities, are they purely coincidental or not?

Refer back to the list of ten high-paying jobs from page 16 and decide whether each is primarily selling a product or a service. Specify who is the market or intended group of consumers for the products or services listed.

Product/Service	Market or Intended Group
1)	
2)	
3)	
4)	
5)	
6)	
7)	
8)	
9)	
10)	

Let's take a closer look at your list to determine your connection to these high-paying positions.

Ask yourself the following:

1) Do you use any of the products or services from this top-ten list? In other words, are you a part of this profession's market?

Provided so,

2) When was the last time that you made use of the product or service?

3) How often do you make use of the product or service?

4) Do you or does your family personally know of anyone who sells any of the products or services you listed?

Find ten real names associated with the top-ten professions you listed. Research as best you can, when and how this person got started. Did they start from nothing, or receive help along the way? If they received help, what type of help?

LIST OF 100

Everybody has to work for a living. The trick is to get paid a whole lot of money for doing something that you would still do even if no one paid you.

Of the List of 100, go through and count how many of these types of professionals that you have actually seen or met in "real life." Where were you and what were the circumstances?

Additionally, if you had to explain each of these 100 positions to a local kindergarten classroom, could you in plain, simple terms say what each of these professionals do?

If not, do not take it as a slight of what you do not know, but take it as a powerful reminder that there are so many different ways in which you can make a living. There are lliterally, numerous worlds waiting for you to explore.

For those positions that you are unfamiliar with, you should know by now what we're going to ask for you to do; that's correct! Look them up and write them down in Chapter Overdrive as something you would like to learn more about (section "b") located in the back of this workbook.

It's time to analyze the "List of 100." Read the following list and pick three entries that intrigue you the most for the questions that follow.

LIST OF 100

1) meteorologist 2) air traffic controller 3) court reporter 4) landscaper 5) climatologist 6) park ranger 7) paralegal 8) nurse 9) cable television installer 10) librarian 11) architect 12) website designer 13) journalist 14) pilot (commercial or private) 15) metallurgist 16) school teacher 17) automotive mechanic 18) car salesman 19) oil rigger 20) police officer 21) university professor 22) real estate agent 23) firefighter 24) copy editor 25) graphic designer 26) fast food franchisee 27) painter 28) carpenter 29) wedding planner 30) plumber 31) construction contractor 32) studio engineer 33) home inspector 34) taxi/limousine driver 35) occupational therapist 36) speech pathologist 37) mortgage broker 38) park ranger 39) mechanical engineer 40) stock trader 41) personal trainer 42) postal worker 43) IT specialist (information technology) 44) insurance broker 45) biologist 46) physician's assistant 47) tailor/seamstress 48) forestry technician 49) geologist 50) optometrist 51) pharmacist 52) psychologist 53) urban planner 54) social worker 55) accountant 56) archeologist 57) special educator 58) private investigator 59) electrical engineer 60) consultant 61) photographer 62) make up artist 63) anthropologist 64) computer repair technician 65) mediator/dispute resolution specialist 66) copy writer 67) locomotive engineer 68) fisherman 69) oceanographer 70) sound technician 71) caterer 72) banker 73) restaurant chef 74) language translator 75) security specialist 76) meteorologist 77) appraiser 78) statistician 79) botanist 80) television/movie camera operator 81) water technician 82) hotel manager 83) import/export broker 84) clinical researcher 85) chemist 86) welder 87) television news anchor 88) aviation mechanic 89) travel agent 90) massage therapist 91) switchboard operator 92) event planner 93) disc jockey 94) public relations specialist 95) museum curator 96) crane operator 97) tour guide 98) beautician 99) barber/hair stylist 100) civil engineer

The three Careers that interest me the most are:

_____   _____   _____
a   b   c

Which Career is listed twice? See the Answer Key on pg. 25!

Advanced

Who works "harder": a CEO of a software company or the janitor who cleans the office space where the software company is located? Additionally, who would you say has the "harder" job?

K E Y   Q U E S T I O N

Many Young Adults simply have no earthly idea of what they wish to pursue as a Career. Why do so many spend so little time working out what they will spend the rest of their life working on?

Now that you have read through the "List of 100" and picked the three most intriguing job titles, answer the following for: (a) (b) (c)

1) What is the typical salary range?

(a)

(b)

(c)

2) What type of Education/degree/certification is needed?

(a)

(b)

(c)

3) How long does it take to get started after high school?

(a)

(b)

(c)

4) How many hours a week does this job require?

(a)

(b)

(c)

Based upon what I know so far, the one profession I would choose for now is (circle one): (a) (b) (c)

Intermediate

Define product in your own words:

A product is:

Similarly, define service in your own words:

A service is:

of a successful product or service?

Advanced

Pick a product or a service that you would not mind selling. Research the market (e.g., who and where are the potential customers/clients) and develop a marketing plan for the product or service.

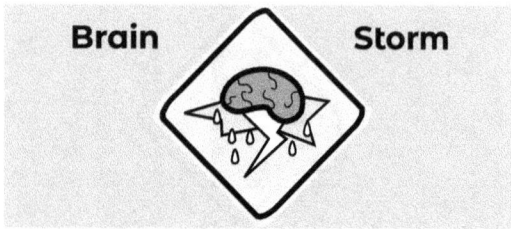

Brain **Storm**

BRAIN STORM

Brainstorming will reveal excellent sources of Career inspiration. The harder you brainstorm, the bigger the rainbow (and pot o'gold) that follows. These ten entries, if answered truthfully, will lead you closer to your destination. List no more than three answers for each.

extra-curricular activities in which you participate (school)

favorite book/story/comic book characters

role models or "really cool" people older than you

hobbies, or things you like to do outside of school

things that your friends and family say that you do better than anyone else

things you daydream about

favorite family past-time

products that you use the most

"extraordinary" television or movie roles you admire

things you do that never seem to bore you

Connecting the Dots

Look at your responses above -- do you see any trends or patterns? What themes keep appearing? Take all the responses, write them down separately and show a third party. Ask them, "What type of person is this? What type of job would they have?" and see if they tell you what you also know to be true.

Ready? We are about to build a new understanding of our relationship with work. We are constantly told to "get good jobs" and "have successful careers," but are those two statements one and the same?

JOB vs. CAREER

Job = typically refers to a short-term solution for your immediate financial needs

With a job, you sell your TIME to the market.

Career = represents a long-term occupational commitment within a defined industry or trade and is typically more open-ended with respect to Career trajectory and compensation

With a career, you sell your KNOWLEDGE to the market.

STOP

Do you agree or disagree with this distinction? Determine your position, circle your answer below and then explain briefly why or why not:

I agree	I disagree

Refer back to the list of products and services from page 16. Select one of the products or services and compare and contrast at least THREE different competitors who sell the same good or service. Try to select competitors who are at the forefront of their fields or industries.

What makes the industry leader in your opinion the best? In what ways do they distinguish themselves from the competition?

KEY QUESTION

What is the fundamental difference between a JOB and a CAREER?

The difference between a JOB and a CAREER is the difference between EXISTING and LIVING. Do you agree or disagree? Explain why, or why not and how?

Develop a product/service to compete with your competitors listed from the Intermediate Exercise on this page. Armed with your market research, make a pitch to your folks; would they buy it or not?

JOB VS. CAREER ACTIVITY

Look at the following positions and decide on its status; then explain the reason for your answer in the analysis section:

Whenever we ask "Why?" we are essentially asking for your "analysis" or rather for you to explain the reasoning behind your reason.

Based upon the JOB and CAREER definitions on page 21, fill the "Analysis" section to your right by asking yourself:

"What primarily is being sold here?"

"Is it time? Or knowledge? If knowledge, then knowledge of what?"

HINT:
JOBS usually earn income through the sale of your time

CAREERS usually earn income through the sale of your knowledge and applied information

(1) video store clerk   ☐ Job ☐ Career
Analysis:_____
_____

(2) movie ticket taker   ☐ Job ☐ Career
Analysis:_____
_____

(3) architect   ☐ Job ☐ Career
Analysis:_____
_____

(4) grocery stocker   ☐ Job ☐ Career
Analysis:_____
_____

(5) NFL Player   ☐ Job ☐ Career
Analysis:_____
_____

(6) dir., after-school programs ☐ Job ☐ Career
Analysis:_____
_____

(7) author   ☐ Job ☐ Career
Analysis:_____
_____

(8) air traffic controller   ☐ Job ☐ Career
Analysis:_____
_____

For the eight positions listed above, on a separate sheet of paper, explain how you could convert each into an entrepreneurial experience.

WHAT VS. WHO YOU KNOW

If you were the "boss" (of which you will be one day), which would you rather have: an employee ranking high in competency or compatibility? Briefly explain what each means.

If you had to rate yourself (of which you will have to each day), which would you say are you better at: competency or compatibility? Briefly explain why.

Word Block

If you're wondering what in Sam's name does competency and compatability have to do with anything, well, here it is:

The truth of the matter is, most people are either hired, fired, or leave due to one or both of the above factors just not being in sync. While some people get along great with others on the job, they simply are unable to fulfill their responsibilities due to lack of training and experience.

Meanwhile, others can handle their responsibilities, but can't get along -- or don't want to get along -- with others on the job. Bear these two factors in mind as you begin to interact with the open market.

Recall, you are interviewing your employer just as much as they are interviewing you. Just because they may give you money, do not forget to ensure that your potential employer is both competent and compatible with your needs above the promised paycheck.

Develop a list of several interview questions that you anticipate hearing at an upcoming job interview. Practice saying the responses out loud verbally so that your responses become more fluid and smooth.

Advanced

WORKING DOUBLE-TIME

We just spoke about choosing a Career over a job. Now, the next strategy we heavily endorse is the deliberate planning for at least two Careers. Why? Well, times change and so do people – and so might your Career goals. Here is what we mean by two Careers:

Career #1 = training-based; receive tutelage and direction in exchange for a FIXED salary or wages

Career #2 = entrepreneurial-based; apply prior training within the free market in exchange for an OPEN-ENDED income

Intermediate

How many entrepreneurs do you know personally or locally?

Make a chart that includes their names, the name of their business and the products or services that they sell or provide.

Next, estimate their annual income or total sales!

How did you arrive at the number you decided upon?

What factors influenced your decision?

With the list of eight positions listed on page 22, first determine which professions are related and identify which would go under the appropriate column, Career #1 or Career #2.

Career #1	Career #2
1)	
2)	
3)	
4)	

KEY QUESTION

Does pursuing two CAREERS really make any sense?

If not, what ONE job or Career can you envision keeping forever? Although you are only blessed with one LifeTime, why not double your chances for future success?

Advanced

You know what's coming: Yep! Interview time! Ask some local entrepreneurs 5-10 "non-threatening" but important questions such as "How long have you been in business?" "What is the hardest part about your day?" to learn more about the demands of entrepreneurship.

CEO OF YOU, INC.

All righty then! With all this talk of going into business for ourselves, it is just about high time that we did so! We are going to create our own business right here and now! This is not to say that you are not free to start another business or still seek another job or Career, but from this day forward, you are now into the business of making YOU grow successful.

What is the name of your business?

What is your motto? (one sentence)

Explain your motto:

Draw your logo:

Word Block

What does this word mean?

entrepreneurship is:

Often, when we work for ourselves, we must work harder than if we worked for someone else. Why do you think entrepreneurship might be harder work?

ANSWER KEY (p.18)

meteorologist

"Everything that glitters is not a golden cash cow!" List ten hazzards or significant risks to becoming an entrepreneur. This exercise is not meant to emphasize "the negative," but to have you anticipate potential bumps in the road ahead.

Advanced

ASK YOUR FOLKS

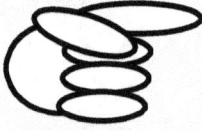

Find out whether or not the current employment position of your parents was the result of choice or chance.

But wait! Before you go ask, based upon what you know and have observed so far, what do you think? Circle your answer below. If Mom & Dad are not available, ask the next responsible adult in your life.

My Mother is currently making money in their position due to:

CHOICE   CHANCE

My Father is currently making money in their position due to:

CHOICE   CHANCE

HEY! Don't let them off the hook! Demand concrete answers! Ask them to share their story (whether painful or pleasurable) about how they ended up where they are today. Is it the result of focused determination? Divine providence? Heartbreak and frustration? Given what they know now, what, if anything, would they do differently?

The Bottom Line

Rearview Review

Smile! We now have a better picture of the road ahead. Reviewing the decisions you made at the various Flash Points throughout the **Career** chapter will lead us to your first **Decision Point**.

Out of 100 Career choices, the one I am most interested in is:

fill with choice from page 8, or insert your own

I will sell my time/knowledge to the market doing the following:

based upon question on page 10, how would you like to get paid?

For training purposes, I plan to gain experience in exchange for a fixed salary for my First Career so that I can ultimately do what I really want for my Second Career. If I had to make a decision today, based upon my answers in this chapter, I would start off doing:

fill in First Career in the box above, fill in Second Career in the box below

I have successfully reached my 1st Decision Point!
I want to work as:

ROADMAP CHECK

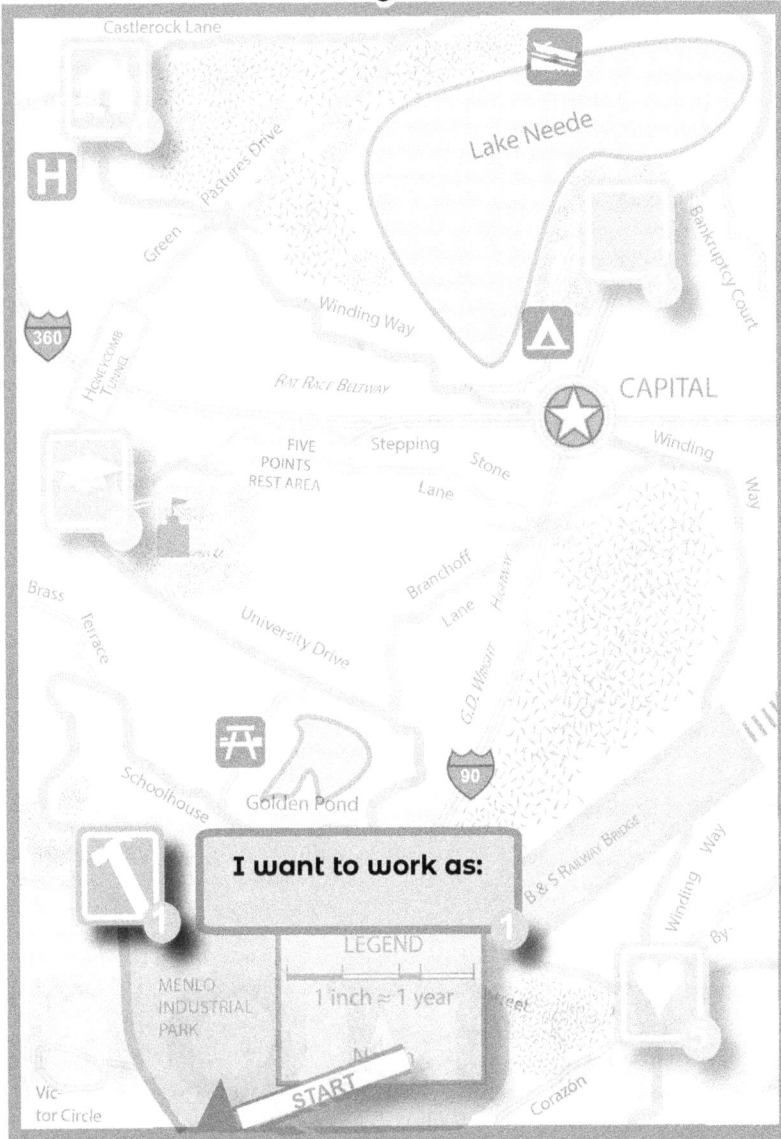

Fuel for Thought

What would you be willing to pay thousands for the chance to make hundreds of thousands?

Alas! The old adage is true: "It takes money to make money." Do not be afraid to spend money or invest time on your future Career; just be sure to spend wisely...

Congratulations!
Now that you have successfully reached this Decision Point, you have unlocked a bonus SIGN OF THE TIMES

Expert Ahead

By planning ahead, we expect for you to become expert in what you will contribute to the biggest race in town -- the human race!

Fill in your "bottom line" DECISION for **Career**. You reached this **Decision Point** based upon the information that you gave yourself so far. Tear this page out or re-write this decision on something that you can carry with you at all times so that you do not forget it.

Recall that your Roadmap is written on paper, not in stone! You may change the above responses at any time. It is better to first make a decision and then make changes, than never to make a Roadmap at all...

Connect   the Dots

EDUCATION

THE ROAD AHEAD

Seeking Guidance

Know the Letter of the Law

Classified Information

The Old College Try

Pipe Dreams

Castlerock Lane

Lake

Pastures Drive

Green

Winding Way

FIVE POINTS REST

Stepping

Stran

Brass

Terrace

University Drive

School House

Golden Pond

Road

G.D. Wooten House

LEGEND

1 inch = 1 year

MENLO INDUSTRIAL PARK

START

Winding

Coranton

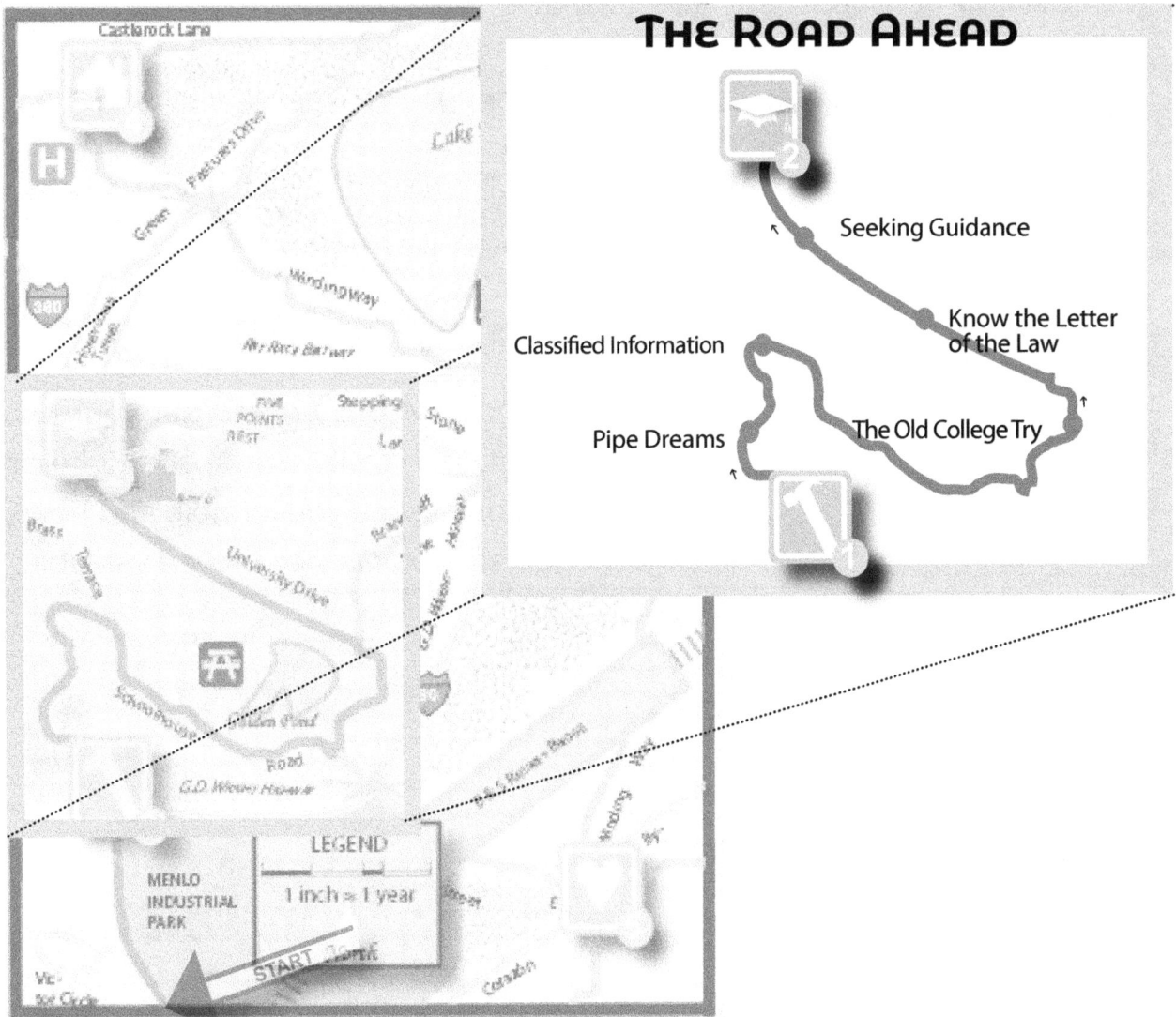

📷 List of Can't Miss Scenes to Capture in this Chapter 📷

1. The understanding that you will make a living based upon specialized knowledge.

2. An acknowledgement that college is not for everyone, yet it is a good place to jumpstart your career options.

3. Effective tools to test which school choices fit you best.

4. Exercises to test whether you have what it takes to get into an institution of higher education.

5. Specific strategies for approaching and enlisting others to assist you in your quest for higher education.

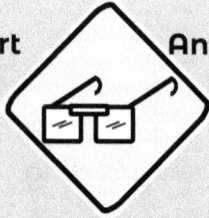

Expert Analysis

List the five (5) things that you have an interest in learning at an expert level (from page 14), then consider the questions that follow:

1)

2)

3)

4)

5)

Now list which majors or areas of concentration in college would match up best with the above interests:

1)

2)

3)

4)

5)

KEY QUESTION

"Education" does not necessarily mean a formalized school setting. Discussion: what other forms can the Education process assume?

PIPE DREAMS

Before we go any further, let's get your "Expert Opinion" first. In the following space, write a time when someone asked you for help and how your knowledge and experience proved valuable:

Recall the moral of the "Pipe Dream" story in Chapter 2 in the It's LifeTime! handbook: if you "know your pipes" inside and out, people will pay you a hefty premium for that knowledge.

Think of an expert in any of the five fields you selected above to your left and answer the following: "How much time does this person spend studying and perfecting their craft when 'off duty'?"

Hey y'all! Although the bulk of this chapter discusses strategies useful in planning for college, we also wish to say that not everyone needs to go to college. In either case, what you need is a plan, or a Roadmap to get going.

On the dotted line below, list the name someone you know who attended college and is now successful -- as you define it:

• •

a. Where attended?

b. What studied?

c. What are they doing now?

On the dotted line below, list the name of someone you know who did not go to college and is now successful -- as you define it:

• •

a. Where did they learn their craft?

b. Who/what helped them study?

c. What are they doing now?

Perform your own research -- don't just settle for what other people tell you!

Create a chart with several measurable metrics (e.g., income, years employed, etc.) and research U.S. Census data to determine whether having a college degree makes a difference in people's lives.

To challenge yourself, research how many of our nation's national U.S. Senators and Congressmen and Congresswomen DO NOT have college degrees.

Now think of someone who did not go to college but has achieved a lot of "success" in their lifetime. Now the catch is, this person must NOT be in the sports or entertainment industry...

If you were honestly looking for a job today, where would you start your search?

If online, which websites do you trust as having reliable information? What do you think of your chances in landing a job with individuals that you have never met before and only met you through your stated past job and Education experience and numerical grade point average listed on your résumé?

In addition to or in lieu of the internet, what other sources can you think of for job leads?

KEY QUESTION

How easy is it to find a job? Let alone a high-paying job? Or a job that you really like?

CLASSIFIED INFORMATION

This next exercise might literally change your life! First, find a recent, local newspaper:

Look through the jobs and opportunities listed in the classified section and answer the following:

Which jobs appeal to you? List at least three:

1.

2.

3.

Do any job listings appear untrustworthy or unappealing to you? Which and why?

For the high-paying jobs that you located, what type of experience is requested and for how long? Are any certifications specified?

In light of the potential areas of study you recently selected, now research possible volunteer opportunities in your field. Where can you give your time today in order to gain experience that will last you a lifetime?

For the job listings that appealed to you, is it absolutely necessary to attend college in order to present as the best candidate? Why or why not?

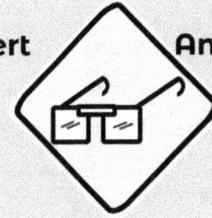

Expert   Analysis

If you are not interested in attending any higher education institution or feel that you are unable, pretend you graduated yesterday, celebrated last night and are now looking at the classifieds now that you are "on your own." Answer the following:

(1) What good/service will you sell?

(2) Do you have to undergo training or can you start right away?

(3) What will be your pay?

(4) Can you do this for the rest of your life?

Based upon your Career interests, what degree (and major) should you choose?

What kind of graduate schools are applicable to your Career interests? For which areas of study?

What additional skills are you looking to acquire in college that you would not otherwise acquire starting work straight out of high school?

What additional experiences are you seeking to gain from your anticipated time in college (e.g., study abroad, sports, clubs & associations, student government, frat life, etc.) besides your degree?

Find someone you know who recently graduated from your current level. Prepare for the interview using some of the same questions that you had to answer here in this chapter. Grill them to see whether and how they will plan out future decisions.

Intermediate

You do not have to "reinvent the wheel"!

Research whether any local or community organizations are sponsoring trips to colleges or universities -- whether it be during winter break, spring break or over the summer.

Depending upon the program, you may have to pay a nominal fee or you may receive sponsorship. Some schools are willing to pay for prospective students to visit them -- all you have to do is invest a little bit of time researching to figure out which ones!

Find at least three college tours for which you are eligible and discuss these tour options with your folks.

THE OLD COLLEGE TRY

Now are you thinking about college? List your top three choices in the boxes on page 35 and then take the mini-quiz below to see how much you know so far. Hey! Don't get mad, just get some answers on that chart!

1. city/state where located

2. nationally known for

3. school mascot/colors

4. annual tuition

5. how many students attend

6. graduate degrees offered

7. average SAT score

8. average GPA

9. average class size

10. expert professor(s)

Advanced

Plan and schedule a campus visit to the closest school on your preferred list. Arrange for a tour and stop by the Admissions Office armed with the answers to these questions and ten more questions of your own.

TAKE-HOME SERIOUSLY Q U I Z

How Well Do I Know
My Top College Choices?

a	b	c

Don't take our word for it, ask your folks! Ask them which three colleges they would recommend for you and don't forget to include the magical question "Why?" and see what they say. Compare their choices to your own to see what is consistent.

Advanced

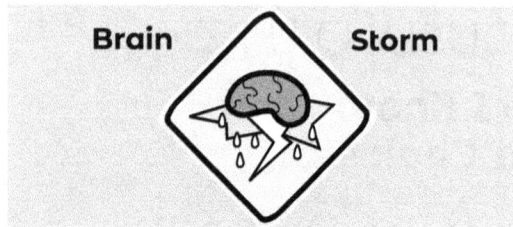

Brain   Storm

RATING SYSTEM
1 = absolutely essential
2 = neither here nor there
3 = haven't really thought about it

BRAIN STORM

In selecting a college, what key factors will you bear in mind? Below, you will find a list of 20 reasons that may influence your top college choice. In the adjacent circle, rate the reason's importance to you:

◯ particular professor

◯ price/tuition

◯ special program or department

◯ resources

◯ research interest

◯ national reputation

◯ party school

◯ place to meet people

◯ good sports teams

◯ student athlete

◯ saw it on TV

◯ close to home

◯ nice campus

◯ friends will attend

◯ alumni in the family

◯ scholarship

◯ distance from home

◯ business opportunities

◯ highly recommended

◯ future spouse

Connect the Dots

What school qualities are missing from the Brain Storm above? If you were a school guidance counselor for a day, what would be the three most important qualities that you would emphasize?

PUT ME ON THE MAP ACTIVITY

Look at the map below and label the map in the following manner.

⭐ = *Capital*   **H** = *homebase*

1 = *top college choice #1*
2 = *top college choice #2*
3 = *top college choice #3*

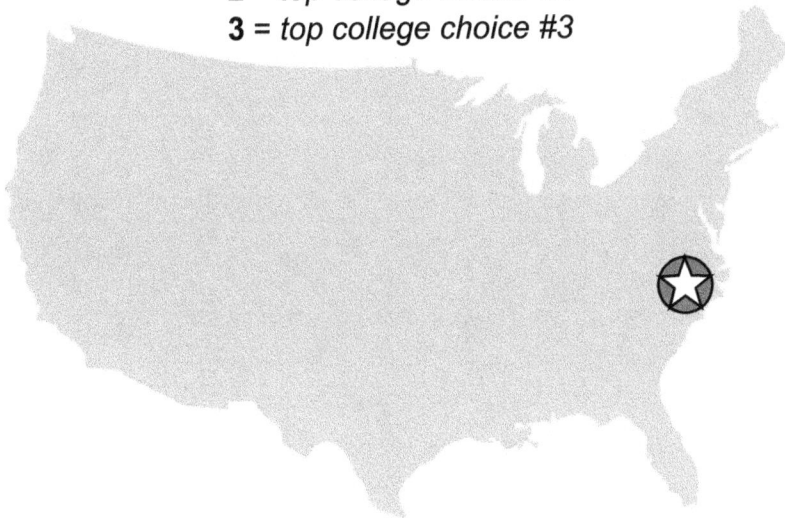

Where specifically are the locations of your top college choices?

Are your top college choices near or within the state where you ultimately wish to live after college? Label where you wish to move as **M** .

How draw lines from your top college choices to   . For your #1 college choice:

The approximate distance in miles:

It will take _____ hours to get home and the average cost will be $ _____ via _____.
(plane/train/bus/car)

I will likely travel home _____ times a semester or _____ times a year.

Map out a possible route to visit in-state or nearby schools on your list of possibilities. Aside from a formal tour, are there any upcoming events where you can "drop in" to see what the vibe on campus is like?

Intermediate

Many schools have different tuition rates for different students. For instance, graduate students pay a different fee from undergraduates, students who stay on campus with a meal plan pay a different fee than those who live off campus, etc.

For starters, determine any differences in tuition for in-state vs. out-of-state residents. The rules vary, but typically you are considered an out-of-state resident if you have not established residency for a year prior to beginning the application process.

If this applies to you, how will the difference affect your decision? Will it increase the amount of your school loans? Does it make sense to apply, take a year off and then move? Conversely are there special scholarship opportunities for in-state residents?

Advanced

Intermediate

Research the difference between the following educational institutions and what degrees/certifications can be earned from each other.

(1) Community/Junior College

Deg./Cert.:

(2) Professional School

Deg./Cert.:

(3) University

Deg./Cert.:

(4) Vocational Institute

Deg./Cert.:

(5) Liberal Arts College

Deg./Cert.:

B.S.

M.A.

B.A.

J.D.

PhD

M.D.

M.S.

MBA

Word Block

KNOW THE LETTER OF THE LAW

So, what does it take to get into college? Not to assume the obvious, but let's take the following acronym quiz to ensure that we are on the same page. What do the following acronyms stand for? This list comprises some of the more popular entrance examinations:

1) M C A T

2) G R E

3) L S A T

4) S A T

5) G M A T

6) A C T

What does acronym mean?

TAKING INVENTORY ACTIVITY

As CEO of YOU, Inc., you must take stock of all of your "goods" so you know what to emphasize when "selling yourself" – even if it is only to a college admissions board. Answer the following as best you can:

Have you received any unique or special recognition for work you have done INSIDE of the classroom? Think of anything outside of your report card.

What do you do OUTSIDE of the classroom? School activities? Hobbies? Memberships? Meetings? Clubs? Organizations? Instruments?

What makes you interesting? What makes you tick? What makes you truly unique?

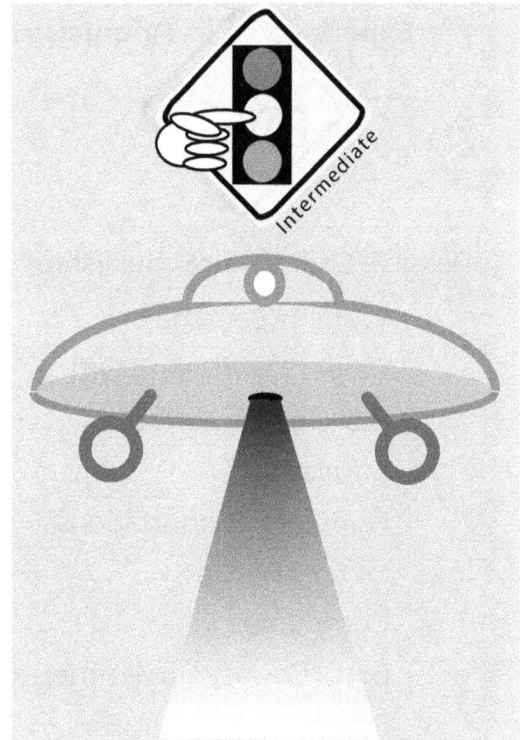

Intermediate

Pretend you are a newspaper reporter and you have been assigned a story whereby someone who looks and behaves just like you was abducted by an alien last night. Aside from the fact that only one cell phone camera captured the alien, there is a lot of talk about the fate of the human abductee. To inform the public about the abductee, you have to write a story about this person. [HINT: the person is you!]

How would you describe this person's interests, talents, positive attributes as well as their value and worth to their community?

Regardless of what grade you are in, request application packets for three colleges. Review questions in the packet and start answering the short answers and essays. Get a third party to edit content. What are the areas you need to work on?

Advanced

Expert   Analysis

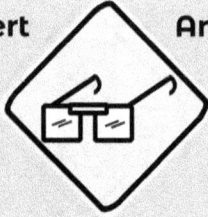

Possible Sources for Scholarships

- Website Searches
- Career Counseling Office
- U.S. Department of Education
- Non-profit Foundations
- Library Books
- Companies
- Local County Government
- State Government
- Local Civic Organizations

Use the information to complete the chart below:

IT PAYS TO BE SMART CHART

Have you spoken with your folks about investing into college? Do your folks have the ability to pay? Or do you need to figure out a way? If so, why delay? Let's start today! On the chart below, list scholarships that you can and will apply for. Feel free to manipulate the chart to add in other relevant details you believe are relevant, such as:

- **the scholarship website address for future reference**
- **formatting requirements (e.g., essay & short answer word limit or page length)**
- **transcript request (official or unofficial)**

It does not matter whether you create the following chart in a word processing document or simply on a sheet of notebook paper. What matters most is that you create an organized system for charting your possible success:

Scholarship Name	Due Date	Eligibility Req'ments	GPA Minimum	Essay Content & Length	Recommendation Requests
1.					
2.					
3.					
4.					

Advanced

Make a list of three individuals who you know and trust to write a favorable recommendation on your behalf. Make contact with them and ask them if they will write one for you in the future and ask them if they need more information about you.

SEEKING GUIDANCE

With all the work that you have done so far thinking about your college choice, it is time to seek out some professional assistance. Have you spoken with your guidance counselor about your college interests yet? If not, try using the script below to introduce yourself and get this all-important conversation started:

Hello Mr./Ms. _____,

My name is _____ and I am in the ___th grade. Here is a list of the teachers and classes I currently am taking. What specific courses should I take if I want a possible career in _____ and WHY? Which colleges are realistic for my academic profile right now? What specifically can I do right now to improve my portfolio?

Thank you,

Again, no guarantees, but while practice does not always mean perfect, it certainly makes for improvement.

Prospective students sometimes know very little about colleges and universities and are just focused on the IDEA of "going to college." We highly recommend performing some more research to make sure the INSTITUTION of college is compatible with your wants and needs.

Ask those around you for their opinion on which college best matches your personality and compare how their feedback resonates with what you are thinking.

For most of these scholarships, you will win money based upon how well you write. Don't like writing, eh? Well, you can't change your height but you can change the way you write! Practice now to perfect your delivery later as your efforts may soon pay off!

ASK YOUR FOLKS

Did your folks attend college or any other institution of higher learning, advanced training or continuing education?

Provided so, quiz them about the following:

- What was your most valuable experience?

- What was your least valuable experience?

- What would you have changed about your educational process?

- What interests do you have that you still wish to study?

The Bottom Line

Rearview Review

Smile! We now have a better picture of the road ahead. Reviewing the decisions you made at the various Flash Points throughout the Education chapter will lead us to your second Decision Point.

1 Out of 5 college majors closely aligned to topics I like, the one I am most interested in is:

fill with choice from page 30, or insert your own

3 After completing the college chart, ranking what is important to me in the BRAIN STORM and seeing how I feel about the distance of the school from home, the top three schools that best fit my needs are:

complete based upon answers from pages 34-37

5 If I had to make a decision today, all other things being equal with respect to financial aid and my academic portfolio, I would attend:

fill with preferred choice from above answer box

I have successfully reached my 2nd Decision Point!

I plan to study and attend:

ROADMAP CHECK

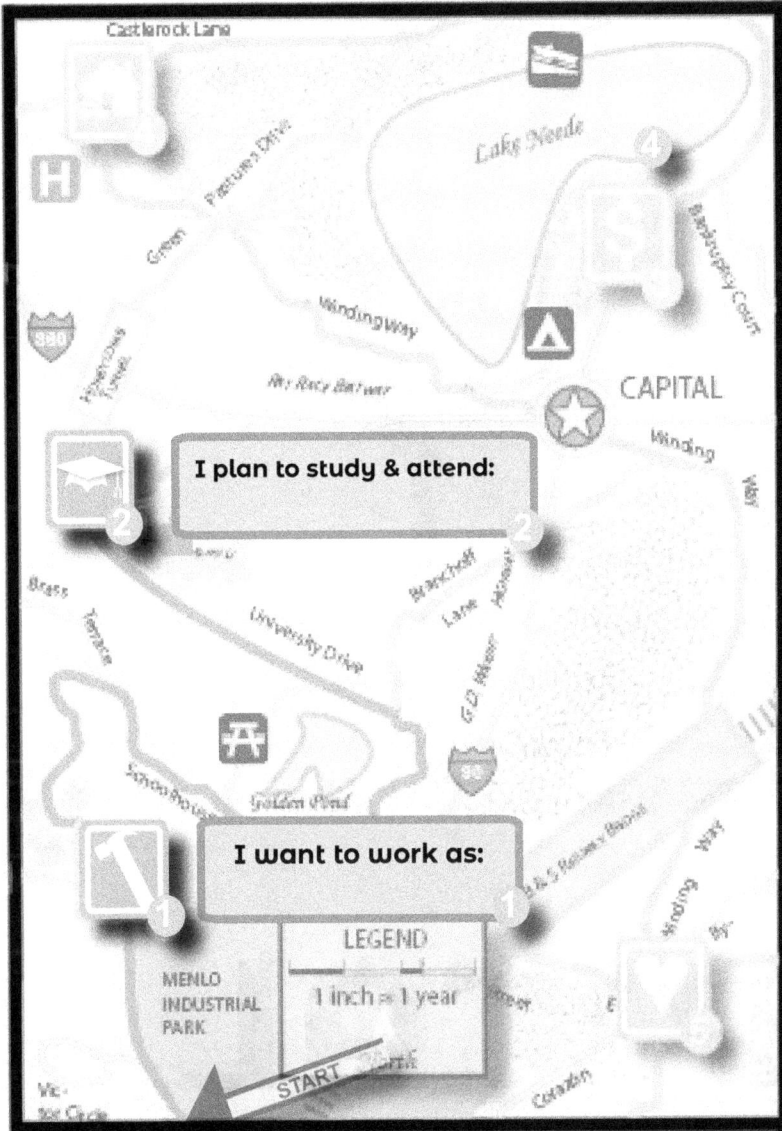

Fuel for Thought

You are never too young to come up with a plan!

Your Education is vitally important! It literally becomes you! Take time WHILE YOU HAVE THE TIME to learn as much as you can. Studying never hurt anyone; only studying too little did.

You do not have to be the brainiest person in the world to be successful; you just have to be smart enough to know what you don't know...

Congratulations! Now that you have successfully reached this Decision Point, you have unlocked a bonus SIGN OF THE TIMES

Athlete / Entertainer Ahead

A cautionary sign, this sign provides pointers for those who do not have a Plan B -- just in case things don't work out...

Connect the Dots

Fill in your "bottom line" DECISIONS for both **Career** and **Education**. You reached these **Decision Points** based upon the information that you gave yourself so far. Re-write these decisions on something that you can carry with you at all times so that you do not forget them.

Recall that your Roadmap is written on paper, not in stone! You may change the above responses at any time. It is better to first make a decision and then make changes, than never to make a Roadmap at all...

CAPITAL

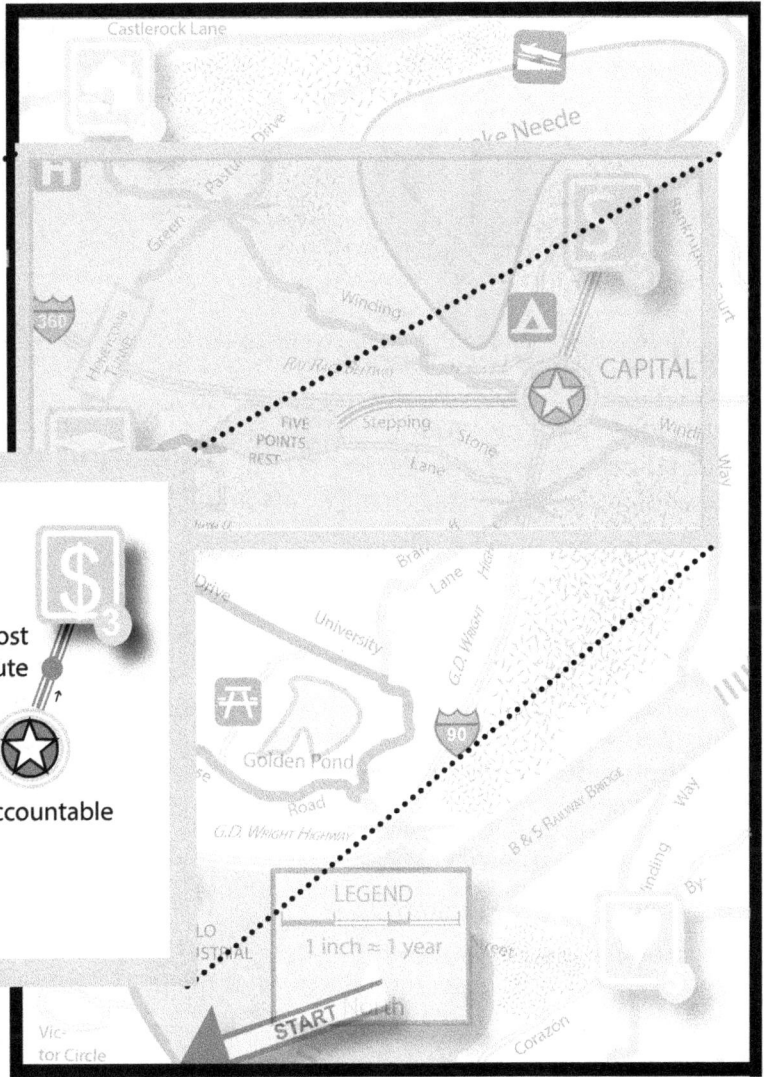

THE ROAD AHEAD

Time to Talk about Money

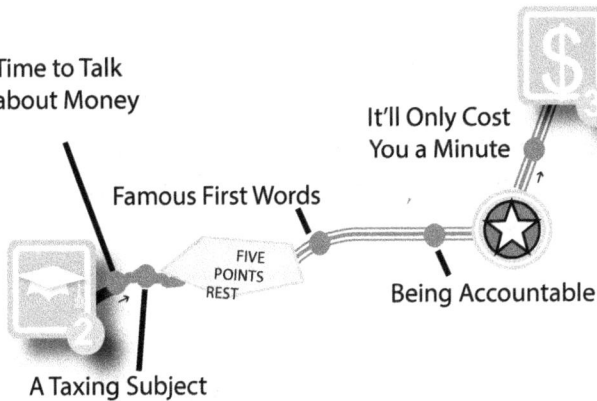

Famous First Words

It'll Only Cost You a Minute

FIVE POINTS REST

Being Accountable

A Taxing Subject

List of Can't Miss Scenes to Capture in this Chapter

1. A candid analysis of the function of money in our increasingly commercial and capitalistic society.

2. How to calculate how much you must pay to "get paid."

3. Tips on how to form a money-making mindset not fueled by greed, but rather driven by a practical passion for success by distinguishing between assets and liabilities.

4. Specific strategies to control your credit before it controls you.

5. Key strategies to evaluate the time you will spend for the money you will make.

Intermediate

Find out where you stand!

Answer the following four questions:

1. **Have you opened a bank account?**
   YES NO

2. **Have you written a check?**
   YES NO

3. **Have you balanced a check book?**
   YES NO

4. **Have you ever looked up a stock in a newspaper?**
   YES NO

If you answered "YES" to all of the above questions, consider yourself on the right track, but challenge yourself and ask which of the above four issues can I learn more about?

If you answered "NO" to any of the above, CONGRATULATIONS! you just disovered something new that you have to learn more about.

Bonus Challenge

Advanced

KEY QUESTION

"Capital" or money, is not everything -- or is it? In our capitalistic society, what can you realistically do without it?

TIME TO TALK ABOUT MONEY

Why do you think people are so shy about declaring that they want to make money?

Why do you think that people find it in poor taste to discuss their salary with strangers?

Is it is harder to discuss money with people who have a lot of money or those who have a little?

What do you consider yourself and/or your family as, lower class, middle class or upper class? Why? Do you have a goal to change your class status? If so, you wish to change to what and why?

Everybody wants to be a millionaire, right? Well find out exactly how many millionaires there are. Use U.S. Census data or newspaper articles as a starting point. Are there more or less than what you thought?

FAMOUS LAST WORDS EXERCISE

"uh, it's not about the money..."

Really?! If somebody says this, don't you buy it for one second!

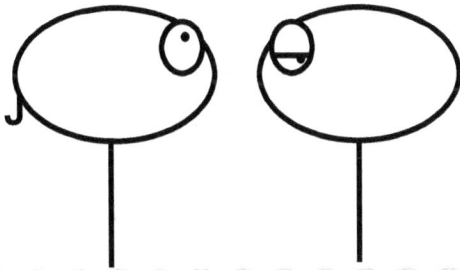

What do people usually say next? That it's about the:

When was the last time you told someone else this phrase? Were you telling the truth?

OK! Enough with all this "money talk" -- tell us when is it ever NOT about the money?

Think about the last time that you gave someone a gift. Is it just the thought that counts or did the amount you spent send a message about how much that person meant to you?

Athlete / Entertainer Ahead

For those harboring aspirations of performing under the bright lights, allow us to be the first to remind you that one day, you will take the stage no longer.

When that day comes, what can you do to generate the same type of income that you did as a star entertainer/athlete once that Career ends?

How does having a college degree affect your post-Career options, if at all?

KEY QUESTION

Have you heard the phrase: "Cash Rules Everything Around Me"? What exactly is meant by this phrase? Does the fact that this phrase originates from a rap song change the meaning of this phrase in any way? Why or why not?

Advanced

Athlete / Entertainer Ahead

For those harboring aspirations of performing under the bright lights sometime in the near future, now is a good time to look into your crystal ball. How long exactly will your career last?

Especially with aspiring athletes, one of the hardest facts to face is that your playing days will one day come to an end (hopefully at your choosing). When that day comes, what's next? What will you transition into? The more you prepare now, the more options you will have later - if and when you really need 'em.

If you have the opportunity to play collegiate sports -- especially on scholarship -- you not only have a unique opportunity to perhaps advance to play professional sports, but you also have an opportunity to obtain a college degree with the aid of a team of professionals dedicated to your success (and your remaining eligibility). It is as amazing as it is alarming how thousands of athlete-students do not fully appreciate or are unable to take advantage of this opportunity to create options.

A TAXING SUBJECT

Before we get too far ahead of ourselves, it is important to take stock of all of this Capital that we expect to accumulate.

Firstly, do you know on average, what the tax rate is for someone like yourself? Have you considered these six deductions?

Federal Tax
State Income Tax
Social Security Tax
Medicare Tax
Employer's Retirement Plan
Employer's Health Care Plan

What do you think (on average) the tax bracket is for the following annual incomes? Draw a line to the correct percentage and then calculate what the actual take-home amount will be. See the Answer Key on page 56:

ANNUAL INCOME		TAKE HOME
a) $7,500	35%	
b) $3.6 M	28%	
c) $93,000	25%	
d) $32,000	15%	
e) $66,000	33%	
f) $300,000	10%	

Advanced

Ask to look at the paycheck of one of your parents. What is their annual salary? How percentage of their monthly salary goes to taxes? Determine the amounts of the six deductions listed above.

PAY YOURSELF FIRST ACTIVITY

Based upon the tax excercise on the previous page, answer the following questions.

Why do people always quote their gross annual income when in actuality they take home significantly less than that after taxes?

When people sit down to compose their personal budgets, which number should they use? The annual salary or their take home pay?

Do you have a plan to pay yourself? If and when you start bringing home income, what percentage are you willing to take away each month for investment or savings purposes? How did you come up with this number?

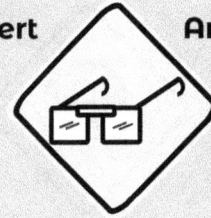

Expert   Analysis

Time to start thinking about developing a financial portfolio!

You don't need to know the exact numbers -- yet -- but reflecting on the contents of your financial portfolio is nonetheless an excellent exercise.

Your portfolio will contain an accurate listing of the following:

Income
Expenses
Investments
Education
Retirement
Tax Liability
Loans
Wills
Trusts
Charitable Donations
Pension
Insurance

If any of the above concepts is "new" to you, then you should look it up!

OK! You pay all of these taxes but where does the money go? To get an idea, research your local county budget since it is a matter of public record. What else besides road maintenance are you paying for?

Brain **Storm**

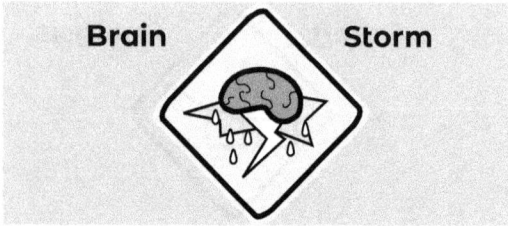

For your Lottery Win Wish List, write down the value/price of ten items you would like to purchase.

Let's take the next step and be specific. For example, if you wrote down "car" as a choice, revise your answer to list the exact car make, model name and year of release. If you put down "expensive watch," again, list both the manufacturer and the exact model name.

Then, research and record the actual cost of the items. Do not forget to calculate the sales tax.

How far off are you from the actual cost?

Is this surprising to you?

Did you overestimate or underestimate the total costs?

If so, by how much?

FAMOUS FIRST WORDS

Have you heard this one before? A guy announces at work: "I just won the lottery!" Everyone cheers and congratulates him but the first thing he says is: "Thanks guys, but I'm not going to change...." OK... but why not change? Isn't that the whole point? Now pretend that you are the lucky lottery winner. List ten items you would purchase with your winnings (and their value/price). Abstract gifts (e.g., "world peace") -- while noble -- are not an option here; think about items that you personally desire.

Lottery Win Wish List

1.

2.

3.

4.

5.

6.

7.

8.

9.

10.

Connect the Dots

Most lottery winners are broke again within two years. Why do you think this is the case? What are the common pitfalls? How would you be different?

WHAT HAD HAPPENED WAS...

You will notice that the last column is without a heading. Label it Asset/Liability. Based upon the definitions to your right, go through your list and label each item as an asset or liability.

Which do you have more of?
How much are your assets worth?
Which asset do you treasure the most?
Which liability is the most expensive?
Which liability do you desire the most?

Word Block

Liabilities
Lose value

Assets
Appreciate in value

Value	Price
Estimated	Actual

Rest assured, you will make money over the course of your LifeTime. The key is not how much you spend, but rather, how much you keep and how much of your possessions keep appreciating in value without you ever "punching a clock"?

Even the humble teacher who "only" earns $35,000 a year will earn over a million dollars over the course of a long career -- provided they work for at least 30 years. The question is how will you leverage the maximum value out of what you will have?

Is this surprising to you? Why or why not?

Go around your house with a pad and pen and compute the value of all of the most significant assets and liabilities that you see. Double-check with your folks to see what you missed.

Intermediate

Take the last item you purchased and dissect the chain of commerce for it:

- Who manufactured it?

- Where else is it sold?

- Who gets to share in the profits?

- Who is the distributor?

- What are the total costs in the price breakdown?

- Where is this product manufactured?

- Is it imported? If so, from where?

BEING ACCOUNTABLE

While we are on the topic of purchasing goods and flexing our consumer muscles, take a brief moment and think about the last time you purchased an item. Did you actually exchange money for products or services? If so, for which?

Did you purchase an essential or luxury item?

What was the amount?

$0-$5 $6-$20 $21-$100 $101+

From where did you originally get the money?

parent/guardian earnings   savings   other

Would you be able to fulfill that need or desire without having the money to purchase that product?

yes   no

Can you think of any other ways in which you may have spent money without spending cash or credit/debit card?

Word Block

In this context, essential means the product/service is vital for your existence and luxury means that you can function without it, no matter how much you like it.

CREDIT CHECK ACTIVITY

It is easy to say "I'm never going into debt" now, but also remember that you are a human being, not a robot. Chances are that at some point in your lifetime, you will owe more than your total worth. In other words, it can happen to you.

So if you are going into debt -- even if just temporariliy -- let's anticipate the value of these potential detours on the road ahead.

What are some items worth going into debt for? Circle the correct letter:

your wedding	y	n
furniture	y	n
certification exam	y	n
college tuition	y	n
car	y	n
home	y	n
dream vacation	y	n
clothes	y	n
private school for kids	y	n
honeymoon	y	n
computer	y	n
business start up costs	y	n

In-debt-pendence Check!

If you do decide to go into debt, consider the following:

(a) Is the item an asset?

(b) Is the item an investment?

(c) Is the item a luxury?

(d) Do you plan to repay?

(e) When will I pay off the debt?

(f) How long will it take me to pay off the debt?

The key is to invest in your future rather than to continue to pay for your past...

KEY QUESTION

What is the fundamental difference between EXPENSES and EXTRAVAGANCE?

Quite simply, it is the difference between what you really don't want but NEED, and what you really don't need, but WANT.

Ask your folks if they have any debt. Ask them if it was accrued acquiring essential or luxury items. Ask them for their advice on balancing the two goals of reducing debt versus making investments.

Intermediate

There are different types of Capital, all of which are not about money.

Below are five forms of Capital identified below:

- Spiritual Capital
- Intellectual Capital
- Economic Capital
- Social Capital
- Emotional Capital

Define what you think is meant by each term. Then rate the five different types above in the order of their importance to do.

Finally, think about how you can increase your investment and dividends in the type of capital you find most valuable.

IT'LL ONLY COST YOU A MINUTE

One future challenge will be figuring out what to do with the Economic Capital you accumulate. In other words, you will have to determine how you will spend your leisure time and disposable income. Define each term:

leisure time is...

disposable income is...

If time is money, then it follows that leisure time and disposable income both function as signs and symbols of wealth. List examples in the chart below:

Leisure Time How would you spend your time?	**Disposable Income** How would you spend your money?
1.	
2.	
3.	
4.	

Advanced

Look closely at both sides of your chart above and determine what, if any, is the total cost of the items and/or activities listed. Can you afford these things currently? If not, how long will it take for you to afford them?

POPPED QUIZ

We are constantly bombarded with messages and images of money -- whether it be from professional athletes' salaries and signing bonuses, gameshow millionaires, or weekly reports of Hollywood movie box office receipts.

But how easy is it to make money?

Based upon your expected salary from your Career choice in Chapter One, how long would it take you to earn the following amounts? Be specific with your description of time:

$0.10

$1.00

$10.00

$100

$1000

$10,000

$100,000

$1,000,000

We are not saying you can't make a million dollars during your LifeTime, but that it may take some time and extra labor to do so. Based upon your Career choice so far, how long will it take you?

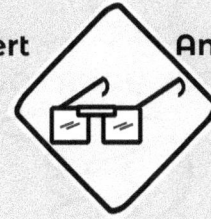

Expert   Analysis

Pretend you have been put in charge of your family for a month. Besides watching all of the TV that you want (just kidding!), you also get to manage the finances.

First, estimate what the total family expenses will be. Think of every category that you possibly can. Next, keep track in a log of expenses the family accrues over the month (e.g., grocery bill, eating out, movie tickets, etc.).

At the end of the month, compare both your estimated and actual expenses to see the differences (if any).

Note: estimated means an educated guess of the item's cost while actual mean the known cost of an item.

Bonus: If your parent/guardian has a budget and is willing to share, compare it with what you came up with.

ASK YOUR FOLKS

When you catch your folks in a good mood, sit them down and ask them the following:

· Do you feel that you have enough Capital? If not, how much more would make you feel 100% secure?

· What is the single-most misunderstood fact about money that you can share with me right now?

ANSWER KEY (p.48)

a) $7,500 = 10%, $6,750
b) $3.6M = 35%, $2,340,000
c) $93,000 = 28%, $66,960
d) $32,000 = 15%, $27,200
e) $66,000 = 25%, $49,500
f) $300,000 = 33%, $201,000

The Bottom Line

Rearview Review

Smile! We now have a better picture of the road ahead. Reviewing the decisions you made at the various Flash Points throughout the **Capital** chapter will lead us to your third **Decision Point**.

In order to accumulate Capital, the percentage or amount I wish to save/invest monthly is:

fill based upon answers from page 49

After completing the Lottery Win Wish List, I see that there are various Possessions that I would like to acquire. In the event I do not win the lottery, I would need this much Capital to acquire everything on my list:

If I had to make a decision today, in light of how long it will

list the total from the items listed on page 51

take me to possibly earn $1M, I would like to start earning this amount annually:

*based upon **Career** choice from Chapter 1, state desired reasonable salary*

I have successfully reached my 3rd Decision Point!

My goal is to earn:

ROADMAP CHECK

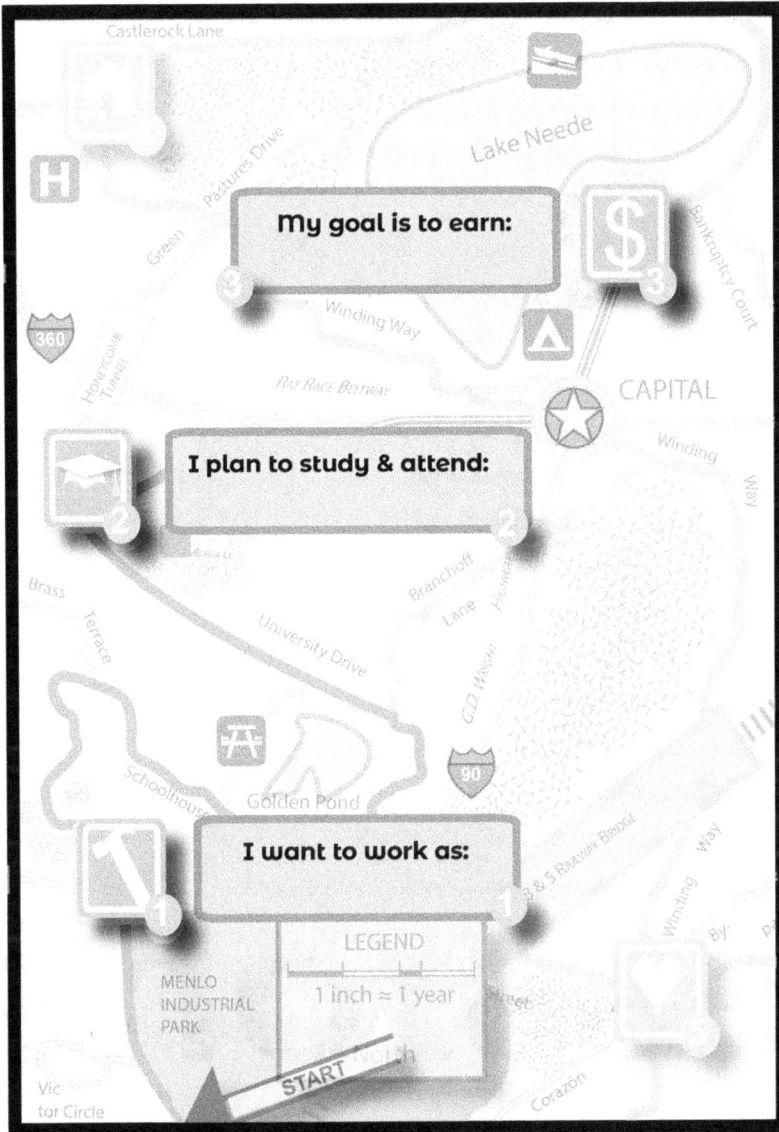

My goal is to earn:

I plan to study & attend:

I want to work as:

LEGEND
1 inch ≈ 1 year

START

Fill in your "bottom line" DECISIONS for Career, Education and Capital. You reached these Decision Points based upon the information that you gave yourself so far. Re-write these decisions on something that you can carry with you at all times so that you do not forget them.

Recall that your Roadmap is written on paper, not in stone! You may change the above responses at any time. It is better to first make a decision and then make changes, than never to make a Roadmap at all...

Fuel for Thought

Capital can stall progress in its absence -- yet it can fuel progress in its abundance! Unless you have an unlimited supply, you will need to figure out how to replenish (and stockpile) your fuel supply. But how ye wonder? Alas! The old adage is true: "It takes money to make money." Do not be afraid to invest money on yourself or your future Career; just be sure to spend wisely... So our question to you is for what are you willing to pay thousands for the chance to make hundreds of thousands?

Congratulations!
Now that you have successfully reached this Decision Point, you have unlocked a bonus
SIGN OF THE TIMES

Black & Brown Xing

For various reasons, many minorities may have different roadblocks to navigate. This sign will help you steer in the clear...

Connect   the Dots

POSSESSIONS

The Road Ahead

You Gotta Pay to Stay

How Can I Be Down?

Would You Buy Your Own House

Driving Up the Price

Sport Utility Vehicle

Evaluating Your Car

(Map labels: Castlerock Lane, Pastures Drive, Green, Lake Needed, Winding Way, Bankruptcy Court, 360, Rat Race Beltway, FIVE POINTS REST, Stepping Stone Lane, CAPITAL, Winding Way, Branchoff Lane, University Drive, G.D. Wright Highway, Golden Pond Road, G.D. Wright Highway, B & S Railway Bridge, Winding Way, By pass, MENLO INDUSTRIAL PARK, Victor Circle, Corazón, LEGEND 1 inch ≈ 1 year, START)

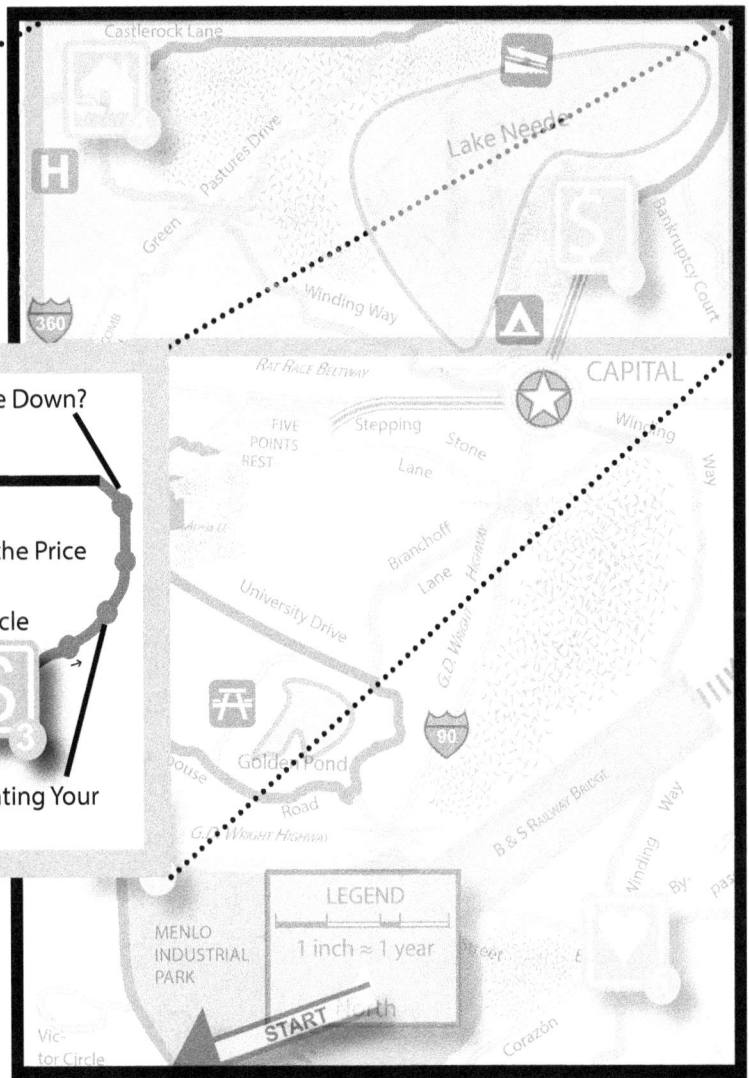

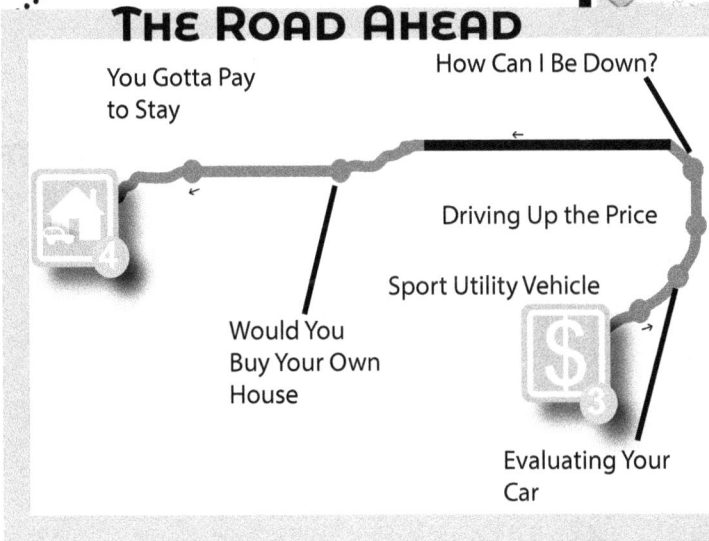

List of Can't Miss Scenes to Capture in this Chapter

1. An understanding that when you make a large purchase, you must balance your needs against your wants.

2. How to analyze whether a car serves you like an asset or a liability.

3. A review of the expenses required to maintain your car.

4. A review of the down payments required to a range of houses.

5. A discussion about what to consider when investing into a home.

6. A helpful review of the accompanying expenses required to maintain a home.

NOTE: We realize that there is more to life than just purchasing a Car or House. However, given the importance placed upon these items as symbols of success and because of the possible repercussions for these two major purchases we focus exclusively on these two items in this chapter.

How much would you expect to pay for the three cars you selected?

Research the sticker price of the version you want -- with all of the desired features included.

> 1.
>
> 2.
>
> 3.

Is it worth it?

SPORT UTILITY VEHICLE

Do you wish to own a car someday? **YES   NO**

List the model and make for three cars that represent your top three choices for what you want.

> 1.
>
> 2.
>
> 3.

OK great! Now choose one of the cars and list the top three qualities you like about it.

> 1.
>
> 2.
>
> 3.

Finally, quickly list three reasons for why you would need a car.

> 1.
>
> 2.
>
> 3.

Do your "likes" and your "needs" match up in the above exercise? Which are more important?

SOCIAL UTILITY VEHICLE ACTIVITY

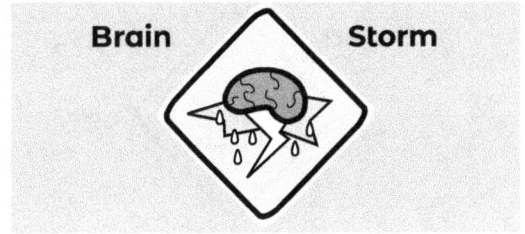

Brain Storm

In addition to the basic necessity of transportation, what else does owning a car mean to you?

Place a check mark in the circles that apply.

○ money

○ confidence

○ "props"

○ respect

○ independence

○ swagger

○ success

○ wealth

○ image

○ status

○ love life

○ pride

Connect the Dots

As much as we say the above do not factor into our decision for transportation, they do. If a lack of Capital prevents you from obtaining your first choice, how can you still satisfy some of the above intangibles?

Expert Analysis

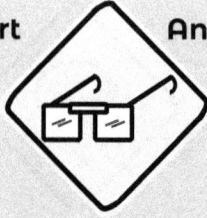

Calculate the monthly car notes for cars with the following purchase prices with an estimated 5% finance charge over 60 months:

$20,000

$40,000

$60,000

If you have trouble with the math, try using an online calculator.

EVALUATING YOUR CAR

Is a car an asset or liability?

How can it be viewed as an asset? How can it be viewed as a liability?

Re-write the following list, ranking the following ten factors in order of their importance for influencing the type of car you will purchase.

Status Statement — 1 — — — — —

Friends' Opinion — 2 — — — — —

Warranty — 3 — — — — —

Gas Mileage — 4 — — — — —

Year & Make — 5 — — — — —

New/Used — 6 — — — — —

Track Record — 7 — — — — —

Size/Seating — 8 — — — — —

Price — 9 — — — — —

Look/Design/Color — 10 — — — — —

Advanced

Ask your folks for some names of some famous athletes and entertainers from the 1980s and 1990s. Research how many still "live lavish," how many went bankrupt and how many still work.

DRIVING UP THE PRICE?

How much are the following semi-regular expenses? Be as specific as you can.

Oil change

Tire rotation

Car wash

Fuel fill up

How often should you perform the following services? List answer in terms of miles or months.

Change air filter

Change spark plugs

New set of tires

New brake pads

Transmission fluid

Change brake fluid

Replace drive belt

Transfer case fluid

Intermediate

Using your top three car choices as "guinea pigs," research what type of warranties are offered by the manufacturer.

What do the warranties cover?

For how long do the warranties last?

Are there any exceptions to these warranties?

For bonus, take the cars listed in the Intermediate challenge above and find out how much monthly insurance would be. What factors or bonuses make a car insurance rate go up or down?

Advanced

Athlete / Entertainer Ahead

Have you ever wondered whether music stars actually OWN the cars and homes you see them with in their music videos?

Percentage of House Price Required as Down payment

HOW CAN I BE DOWN?

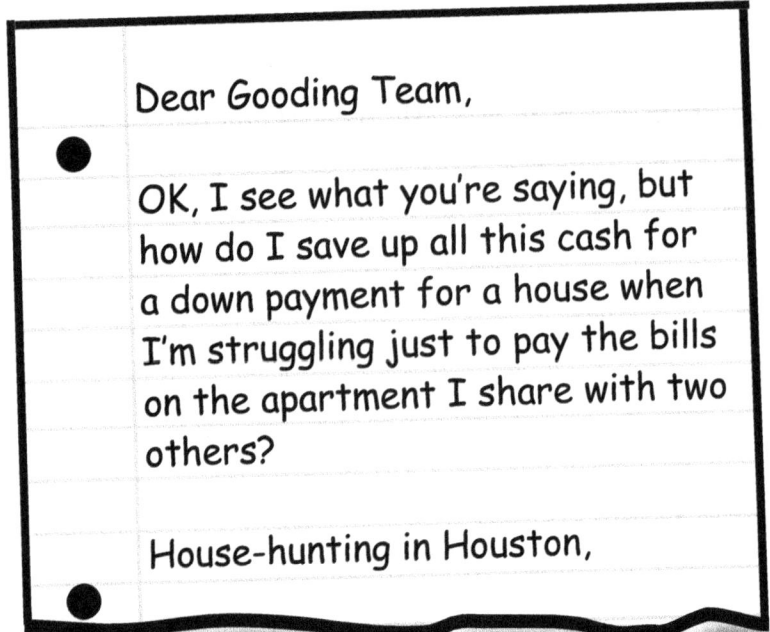

Dear Gooding Team,

OK, I see what you're saying, but how do I save up all this cash for a down payment for a house when I'm struggling just to pay the bills on the apartment I share with two others?

House-hunting in Houston,

This is the million-dollar question. Especially with many lenders frowning upon highly-leveraged mortgages, it has become more difficult. But as with everything else, your chances improve considerably if you have a plan in place. The first step is knowing exactly how much you need.

Calculate the down payment amounts required:

	$250,000	$2.5m
1%		
5%		
10%		
20%		

Go online or grab a free copy of a "home buyer's guide" from your local grocery Browse through either and select a home that you like. Then look at the price. What would you need to do to buy that house?

WOULD YOU BUY YOUR HOUSE?

Using your current residence as a point of reference, answer the following questions. If it were up to you, are there some items that you would like to change? If so, which and why?

How far from where you live is:

Grocery store?

Post office?

Mall/shopping district?

Library?

Hospital?

Airport?

Gas station?

Your neighbor?

Your place of employment?
[use your parents' workplace if you are not working]

Elementary school?

The nearest traffic light?

Fire station?

The nearest street lamp?

These questions all seem corny and like overkill until you move in. These may not be "deal-breakers" but they do not have to be surprises, either.

Before moving in to your new pad, think about "casing the joint" or "hanging out" during the morning and evening to see what the vibe is before you discover that the loud, barking dog is actually your neighbor!

Black & Brown X-ing

Not having generations of wealth to tap into may make a difference, which is why college is an option to seriously consider as a means of achieving material success. If you are African American or Latino, the statistics are sobering indeed where nationally, the high school graduation rates are only about 56%. Additionally, not that many African American or Latino students go on to college because it is either not practical, not affordable or it is not clear what the benefit will be.

If you live in a community or family where college is emphasized as an option, then getting in to college may not be as much of a concern as GETTING OUT of college. Despite how much it may mean to you, without a plan your degree may not mean much in the open marketplace.

If college is not in the cards for you, neither fear nor fret not. With a solid plan, solid focus and consistent execution, you can outearn many college graduates.

YOU GOTTA PAY TO STAY

Compare the difference between your estimates and the actual cost that your parents absorb each month.

Which expenses did you overestimate or underestimate?

In calculating the cost of living, what makes the most amount of sense for your dollars?

When you first break out on your own, based upon your projected Career choice, should you start off in an apartment? If so, with or without roommates?

How will your desired location impact the cost of living expenses that you must incur?

Will a condominium best suit your desires and tastes? What about a townhome? Must you have a single-family residence? If not, what are the alternatives?

Using your current residence as a "guinea pig," what would you estimate are the monthly expenses for the following?

mortgage

property taxes

home insurance

water

electricity

gas

waste removal

phone

internet

cable

landscaping

The following are a bit more abstract in that you do not necessarily receive one singular bill each month for these expenses. Yet, you will likely incur these costs of your time/money just the same:

house cleaning

laundry/cleaners

AC/heating bill

groceries

Ask your folks for a copy of the utilities. If you live in an apartment or condominium whereby certain expenses are included, see if you can dig a bit deeper to find out what the itemization of those fees are.

THE PRICE OF SUCCESS REVIEW

If money were no object, how much would your "dream house" cost?

If it costs $1M dollars, what would be the monthly mortgage due?

How much does your "dream car" cost?

For a five year (60 month) financing plan, what would be the monthly note?

Let's briefly review. At the end of Chapter 1, you stated that you wish to be a:

At the end of Chapter 3, you stated that you wish to earn:

Based upon your projected Career choice and income level, are we in the ballpark for making these purchases possible? If not, what else might you do to make up the difference?

Black & Brown X-ing

More Blacks & Latinos are making more money now than at any other point in American history. The earning power and spending power of these two minority groups has grown considerably over recent years.

Therefore, the income gap between whites and people of color has grown smaller.

However, Blacks and Latinos still lag behind whites on virtually all wealth valuation scales.

Where do you think this gap comes from if we all are equal?

When and how will this gap be bridged?

KEY QUESTION

What is the price of happiness?

Money helps, but it can only buy so much. At the end of the day, what will be the source of your happiness? What will it take to have fulfillment whether you have money or not?

Ask your folks if they own a home or a condominium -- what percentage did they have to pay down? What were the terms and rates? How long did it take for them to save for that payment?

ASK YOUR FOLKS

By now, your folks should have some experience with both assets and liabilities.

Ask them about the following:

- What is the most valuable possession that you have ever purchased? Did you purchase it alone?

- What is the greatest liability you presently have or used to have? How did you or how will you get rid of it?

- Do you plan on passing on any assets to me one day? If so, what can I do to prepare for their transfer?

- Is/was the expense worth it?

The Bottom Line

Rearview Review

Smile! We now have a better picture of the road ahead. Reviewing the decisions you made at the various Flash Points throughout the Possessions chapter will lead us to your fourth Decision Point.

3 After evaluating all of the expenses associated with a vehicle, I aim to spend $____ monthly on this vehicle:

state amount willing to pay monthly for car note from page 63

6 After analyzing the "other" expenses necessary for home ownership, after moving out from my folks, I am most interested in moving to:

review expenses on pages 66-67 and think about where you would like to live

4 If I had to make a decision today, all other things being equal, based upon my Career choice and expected Capital income, I am looking to buy or save up a down payment for a house that costs:

In light of the Advanced activity on page 64, insert a reasonable price

I have successfully reached my 4th Decision Point!

I wish to drive & move to:

ROADMAP CHECK

I wish to drive & move to:

My goal is to earn:

I plan to study & attend:

I want to work as:

LEGEND
1 inch ≈ 1 year

MENLO INDUSTRIAL PARK

START

Fill in your "bottom line" DECISIONS for **Career**, **Education**, **Capital** and **Possessions**. You reached these Decision Points based upon the information that you gave yourself so far. Re-write these decisions on something that you can carry with you at all times so that you do not forget them.

Recall that your Roadmap is written on paper, not in stone! You may change the above responses at any time. It is better to first make a decision and then make changes, than never to make a Roadmap at all...

Fuel for Thought

There is nothing wrong with the acquisition and accumulation of material Possessions -- in fact we encourage it!

The key is to take full ownership of your Possessions -- and not let them end up "owning" you.

Congratulations!
Now that you have successfully reached this Decision Point, you have unlocked a bonus
SIGN OF THE TIMES

No Lolly-gagging

By planning ahead, we expect for you to know what is expected of you and take seriously the responsibility of Possessions.

Connect the Dots

COMPANIONSHIP

THE ROAD AHEAD

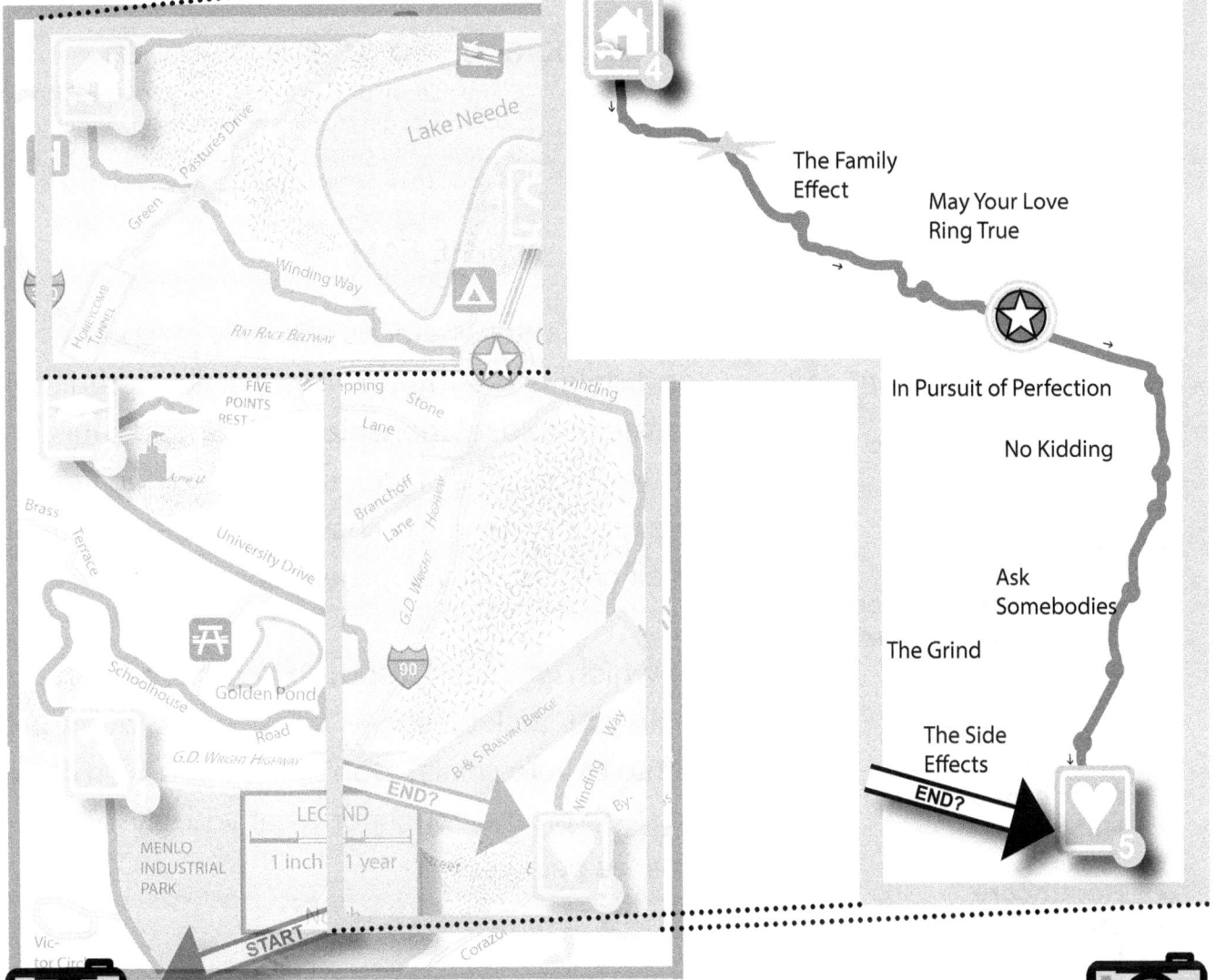

The Family Effect

May Your Love Ring True

In Pursuit of Perfection

No Kidding

Ask Somebodies

The Grind

The Side Effects

END?

Lake Need

Pastures Drive

Green

Winding Way

Honeycomb Tunnel

Rat Race Beltway

FIVE POINTS REST

Stepping Stone Lane

Winding

Brass Terrace

University Drive

Branchoff Lane

G.D. Wright Highway

90

Schoolhouse

Golden Pond Road

G.D. Wright Highway

B & S Railway Bridge

Winding Way

END?

LEGEND

1 inch = 1 year

MENLO INDUSTRIAL PARK

START

Victor Circle

Corazon

List of Can't Miss Scenes to Capture in this Chapter

1. From the mountaintop we see that true love is often borne of true friendship.

2. From the valley we see that as with most things, a good marriage requires hard work.

3. As we reach the crossroads, we will see that romance without finance is a big nuisance.

4. Lastly, at we near the final destination on this Roadmap, we pick up some previews of what parenthood entails -- arguably, the most challenging, yet rewarding part of the journey that awaits you...

NOTE: We do not assume that every Young Adult wishes to get married and/or have children although we support and encourage the decision to do so. We recognize that whether one decides to or not, we humbly suggest that decision will impact other areas of the Young Adult's life in significant ways. Even still, the insights contained in this chapter can be applied to a variety of friendships and relationships, in addition to some "fuel for thought" for those who wish to venture down this road...

Intermediate

Have you considered starting and having a family some day?

How much do you estimate it would "cost" to raise a child all the way until they are eighteen years old?

Items to consider:

- **Baby Gear (pampers, bottles, cribs, car seats & strollers)**
- **Clothes**
- **Food**
- **Schooling**
- **After school activities**
- **Hobbies**
- **Travel**
- **Healthcare**
- **Entertainment**
- **Your Time & Attention (emotional, intellectual and spiritual support)**

1

Advanced

KEY QUESTION

"Companionship" does not necessarily mean that you HAVE to get married or have kids in order to be successful. But guess what? The decision to do so or not to do so will impact you greatly either way.

THE FAMILY EFFECT

In this chapter, we focus primarily on spouse and children -- why? While you undoubtedly will create untold relationships with untold souls, the relationships of your spouse and children are unique in that you have such a central role in their creation, development and maintenance.

In which ways can a spouse and/or children help you "pick up speed" or "slow you down" en route to your goals? Don't worry, you won't have to sleep on the couch for what you say in the spaces below!

1.
2.
3.
4.
5.

How much do you estimate college tuition will be annually by the time your kids would have to go to college?

MAY YOUR LOVE RING TRUE

Some of you may never get married.

Moreover, some of you may never WANT to get married.

In either case, it is what it is.

For those of you who are considering marriage as a future option, answer true or false to the following questions.

People in married couples make more money

TRUE FALSE

People in married couples live longer

TRUE FALSE

People in married couples are in better health

TRUE FALSE

Married persons get promoted faster

TRUE FALSE

Married persons suffer from more violent crime

TRUE FALSE

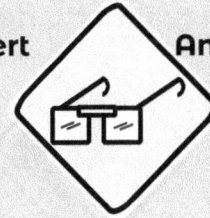

Expert   Analysis

Do you believe in "love at first sight"?

Or do you think that true love, like most truly great things, takes time to develop?

List the pros and cons of an extended courtship.

Additionally, state how long after you meet "your love" would be a reasonable time to wait before marrying.

NOTE: courtship is the exclusive dating of an individual over an extended period of time

Studies show the answers are all TRUE! If you do not believe us, research the answers! As an Advanced activity, this information will be more memorable as you discover it for yourself. Email us if you need help...

Athlete / Entertainer Ahead

For those harboring aspirations of performing under the bright lights, now is a good time to look into your crystal ball.

How might having a family (e.g., spouse and/or children) affect the development of your craft or your ability to practice, perfect and perform?

Would these relationships make your enterprise more difficult or more comfortable?

Get a head start on determining how you feel about this issue -- chances are, your spouse and kids will have an opinion...

Advanced

IN PURSUIT OF PERFECTION

In looking for Mr. or Mrs. Right, have you considered what qualities you are looking for? Aside from "smoking-hot" looks, have you considered how different from you this person could be personality-wise?

Before we move any further, let's take the Perfection Test. List three qualities about yourself that someone else might find annoying (e.g., you absolutely refuse to allow the syrup to touch your eggs on the same plate).

1.
2.
3.

Now explain how these qualities enhance who your personality, and actually add to who you are.

1.
2.
3.

Congratulations! You have taken the first step in maintaining a healthy long-term relationship! The point here is that you simply cannot control other people no matter how much you love them. Just like you defended yourself in the space above, you will also have to defend your spouse's honor even when they eventually remind you that they too are not perfect. Seek perfection together...

How do you respond to conflict? Do you like your "space" and like to take your time to "process" what is happening? Or do you like to immediately confront the problem? Knowledge of this detail may impact your most vital relationships.

LIVING THING TEST

Now it's time to take the "Living-Thing" Test.

Llist three living things that you can care for in or around your home:

_____   _____   _____

If you were in charge of ensuring these three things' survival, how often would you feed them? In other words, quantify in time a reasonable maintenance schedule to keep these things in optimal condition or alive.

_____   _____   _____

Whether it be a houseplant, goldfish, or the front lawn, it behooves you to ensure proper maintenance for your enjoyment and their survival.

Why then take arguably our most important relationships for granted? When it comes to a potential life-long relationship with one spouse, what are three ways in you can care for, feed and invest in the marriage as a "living thing" unto itself?

1.

2.

3.

Have you ever owned a pet?

If so, how difficult was the responsibility of caring for another living thing?

Think of a time where you were "in charge" of other people. What was the most challenging part of getting them to do what you wanted?

THE MONEY HONEY

Have you ever heard the expression that "ain't nuthin' funny without the money?"

One of the leading issues that drives too many couples to an untimely demise is any issue involving cash money, dividends, paper, coin, moolah, greenbacks, dough, scratch, dinero, etc.

Here are some questions to ask to help avoid surprises down the road.

- Do you want to hold separate accounts?
- What are "necessary" expenses?
- What are "unnecessary" expenses?

While these questions may appear to be repugnant and fly in the face of true love and blind devotion, they are also quite practical. Eliminate the guesswork! You have too much at stake. What are some additional questions you can think of that will help you understand how your potential partner thinks about finances?

?

?

?

?

Intermediate

Ask to go to the bank with your folks the next time that they go.

Record your thoughts silently and ask your folks questions about their transaction once complete.

Advanced

Ask your folks to include you the next time they have a meeting about finances at home and take notes!

NO KIDDING

How will having children affect your Roadmap? Well, there's only one way to find out. Be honest (and selfish) about your answers here. Even though you were a kid, that does not mean you have to have a kid later on in life. Let's analyze:

What are the pros and cons of having children early? [Early = before age 30]

PROS	CONS

What are the pros and cons of having children later? [Later = after age 30]

PROS	CONS

Think of and make a list of five individuals who you believe represent success. Next, determine whether or if they were married and/or had kids before or after they established their successful careers:

Person	Married	Kids
1.		
2.		
3.		
4.		
5.		

What about the "wildly successful" people that you see on TV? How are these people's personal lives compare to other successful people you know such as your favorite teacher, preacher or police chief?

Look around your classroom and conduct a poll.

Of your classmates, how many have parents older or younger than yours?

Under the Married and Kids columns, put a "B" for before, put an "A" for after or pit a "N/A" if non-applicable

Intermediate

What does marriage mean to you?

Is it an emotional or business decision to get married?

Is it a contract?

If so, what are the Terms of Endearment or Engagement?

How do you determine a breach of contract?

If a breach occurs, how do you assess damages?

ASK SOMEBODIES

Don't take our word for it, take into consideration the experience of those you know. Find a married couple with children. Below are three key questions we recommend for discussion:

Hello Married Couple,

How long after when you two first met did you realize that you wanted to be married?

When did you decide to start a family (e.g., have kids) and to what degree was it planned?

In retrospect would you do anything different about the timing of your marriage and kids?

Thank you,

Advanced

Is living a "single life" or married life more advantageous to being successful? How many wildly successful examples can you think of where the people are single? With children? Married? Both?

THE GRIND

Ideally, you will open up your own business and will be overwhelmed with plenty of good business after having successfully completed college and professional or graduate school without having to take out any school loans. In the meantime, let's walk through a pretend scenario involving the dreaded "Rat Race."

Pretend you are a college graduate, have nearly $100,000 in total debts and school loans and landed a job paying $35,000 a year and you ABSOLUTELY HATE your job since it has nothing to do with your major in college and you do not get paid for overtime even though you routinely work ten hour days. Let's not forget you are married with two kids and perform both "pick up" and "drop off" duties, leaving you with little spare time to get ahead.

Write down what you would do to find extra time to make extra money. Is it still possible for you in this scenario to become a millionaire without hitting the lottery or doing anything patently illegal? If so, how long will your plan take?

Black & Brown X-ing

Nationally, just about 7 out of 10 babies are born out of wedlock within the African American community.

How might this statistic affect the successful pursuit of the other Decision Points discussed so far?

Which is easier: to find love after finding money? Or or to find money after finding love?

Brain 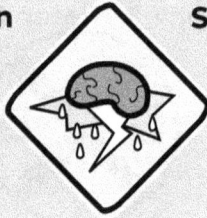 **Storm**

THE TIMING OF KIDS

What's most important to you? In the circle for the events listed below, indicate with an "X" those events that you absolutely cannot miss -- which you *might have to* depending upon your work schedule. Can you think of any others?

First loss of tooth

First day of school

First recital

First karate belt test

First school performance

First fieldtrip at school

First intramural game

First walking steps

Open house at school

First school performance

First time riding a bike

Reading for 30 min. ea. night

First day riding bus to school

First tying of shoe

First Parent Teacher Association Meeting

Classroom volunteer

First trip to doctor

Connect the Dots

How important were the above items to you? Were some more important than others with respect to having your parents participate?

THE SIDE EFFECTS

The "side effects" of having children are that you have to "grow up" quickly and learn how to put their needs above yours.

Real quick! Think of a time when your folks sacrificed something for you:

Age: **Situation:**

Sacrifice:

Out of all of the Decision Points, which do you see as being affected the most with the addition of a spouse?

Which Decision Point would most be affected by the addition of kids? Why?

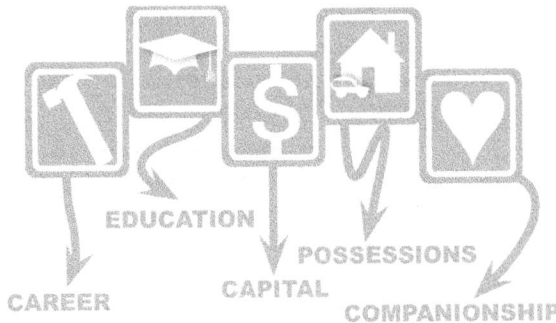

EDUCATION

CAREER   CAPITAL

POSSESSIONS

COMPANIONSHIP

No Lolly-gagging

Meaningful relationships can be very rewarding but very demanding as well.

Ask your folks what is the most challenging part about being a parent and see what they say.

Then ask them what is the most rewarding part about being a parent and see what they say.

Then, if you are able, ask your GRANDPARENTS the same question about your PARENTS to see what they say!

What would you want your children to say about your parenting?

Which of the five Decision Points would you sacrifice first? Which would you absolutely wait to sacrifice last?

Advanced

Intermediate

Write down your morning schedule and routine.

How many steps do you have to go through before you walk outside of the door to "start your day"?

THE SCHEDULE ACTIVITY

>> *You wake up.*

>> *You nudge your spouse and greet the toddler while you change the infant's diaper.*

>> *You jump in the shower.*

>> *You jump out the shower and hurriedly dress yourself.*

>> *You pick out the toddler's clothes and direct your spouse to change the toddler.*

>> *You make up your bed, make up the infant's bed and "help" the toddler make up her bed.*

>> *You make breakfast for the family – really the kids.*

>> *You make new formula bottles for the infant while washing the old ones.*

>> *You make lunch for the toddler.*

>> *You pack lunch for yourself.*

>> *You empty the dishwasher.*

>> *You feed the infant, you brush everybody's teeth (including your spouse's).*

>> *You make pointless protests about "not wanting to be late."*

>> *You load everyone into the car.*

>> *You drop off the infant and the toddler at both preschool and day care (in two different locations).*

>> *You work a full day (and deal with whatever "drama" that happens at work).*

>> *You pick up the kids from day care and preschool.*

>> *You retrieve the mail (read: bills).*

>> *You change out of your work clothes/uniform.*

>> *You take the toddler to dance-enrichment lessons.*

>> *You cook dinner.*

>> *You wait for your spouse's return and dash out to the gym to go "workout."*

>> *You return to wipe down the stove, clean the kitchen table and sweep the kitchen floor.*

>> *You start baths for the kids.*

>> *You put the kids in their pajamas.*

>> *You read the kids a book apiece.*

>> *You put the kids to bed.*

How might you make this above schedule easier and more efficient? Cross out the steps above you deem unnecessary and write down your suggestions below:

Advanced

In which ways can you add to your schedule to make additional progress towards your other Decision Points?

THE END OF THE ROAD?

Congratulations! Other than the Rearview Review that concludes this chapter, this is your final exercise in this workbook-long exercise in critical thinking. You have done yourself proud!

We discussed the following five Decision Points:

1. _____ symbolized by a _____

2. _____ symbolized by a _____

3. _____ symbolized by a _____

4. _____ symbolized by a _____

5. _____ symbolized by a _____

While we posed to you questions that require immediate concern for the construction of your Roadmap, we leave you with some additional questions to bear in mind for the road ahead.

What future contribution do you want to be most remembered for? What would be your ultimate dream accomplishment? What would you like to have done with your LifeTime?

Be honest: which Decision Point strikes you as the most important for you to reach?

Which Decision Point strikes you as the easiest to obtain? Which strikes you as the most difficult?

ASK YOUR FOLKS

Whether your folks are married or not, quiz them about the following:

- How long were you all together before you had me?

- Did you plan to have children? If so, for how long?

- How did having children change your life?

- What surprised you about marriage? Was there anything easier or harder than what you thought it would be?

- With respect to having kids, what advice would you give me?

The Bottom Line

Rearview Review

Smile! We now have a better picture of the road ahead. Reviewing the decisions you made at the various Flash Points throughout the Companionship chapter will lead us to your fifth and final Decision Point (in this book).

Based upon the information in this chapter, it merely confirms my opinion that with respect to getting married, I will:

fill with current preference

Based upon the information in this chapter, it merely confirms my opinion that with respect to having kids, I will:

After completing the contents of this entire workbook,

fill with current preference

based upon the direction of my desired Roadmap and my timetable for doing so, when it comes to marriage and having kids, I will:

if you answered "Yes" for either of the above two, enter preferred timeframe

I have successfully reached my 5th Decision Point!

My preferred status is:

ROADMAP CHECK

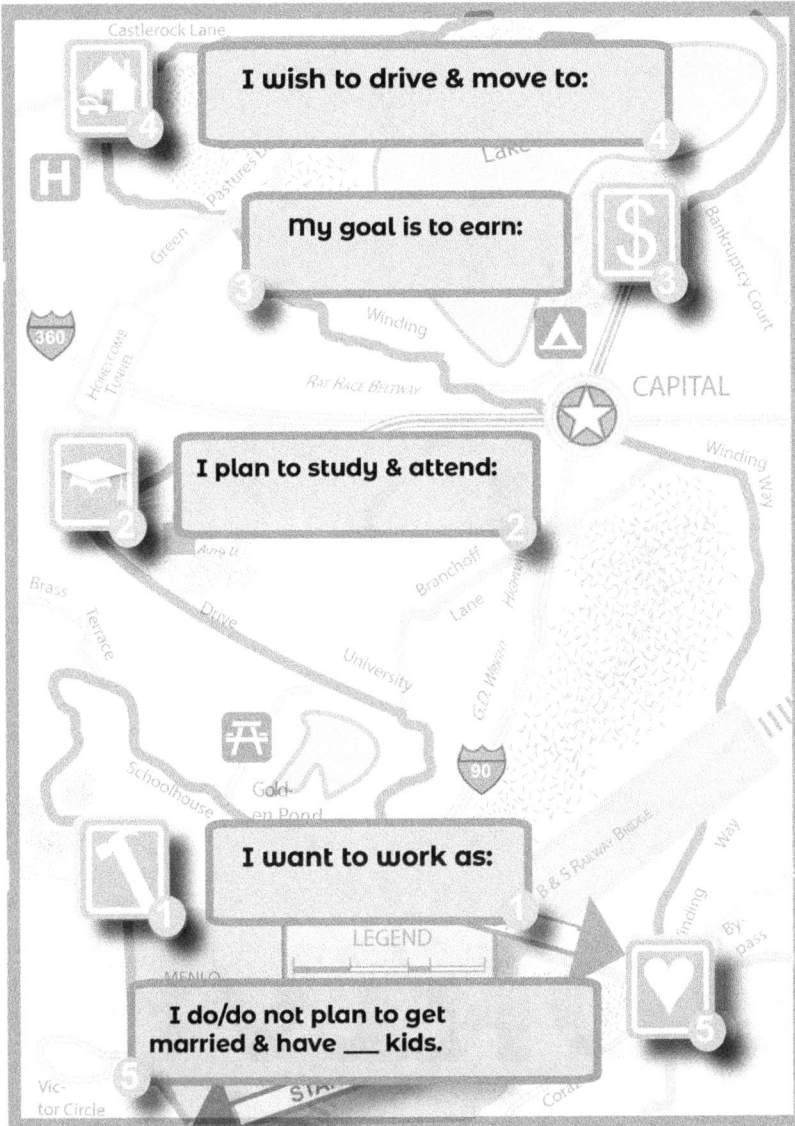

R

I wish to drive & move to:

My goal is to earn:

I plan to study & attend:

I want to work as:

I do/do not plan to get married & have ___ kids.

LEGEND

CAPITAL

Fill in your "bottom line" DECISIONS for Career, Education, Capital, Possessions and Companionship. You reached these Decision Points based upon the information that you gave yourself so far. Re-write these decisions on something that you can carry with you at all times so that you do not forget them.

Recall that your Roadmap is written on paper, not in stone! You may change the above responses at any time. It is better to first make a decision and then make changes, than never to make a Roadmap at all...

Fuel for Thought

While it may not be quite the time for you to get married or have children, it is nonetheless never too early to plan!

You can't plan once you have 'em, so take advantage now to think about where you wish to be in relation to your Roadmap if and when you eventually do.

Congratulations! Now that you have successfully reached this Decision Point, you have unlocked a bonus SIGN OF THE TIMES

Time is Money

By planning ahead, we expect for you to avoid the hazzards of the dreaded Rat Race so that your life may be as interesting and fulfilling as possible. Take time -- while you have the time -- to invest in your future by creating a Roadmap today..

Connect the Dots

OVERDRIVE

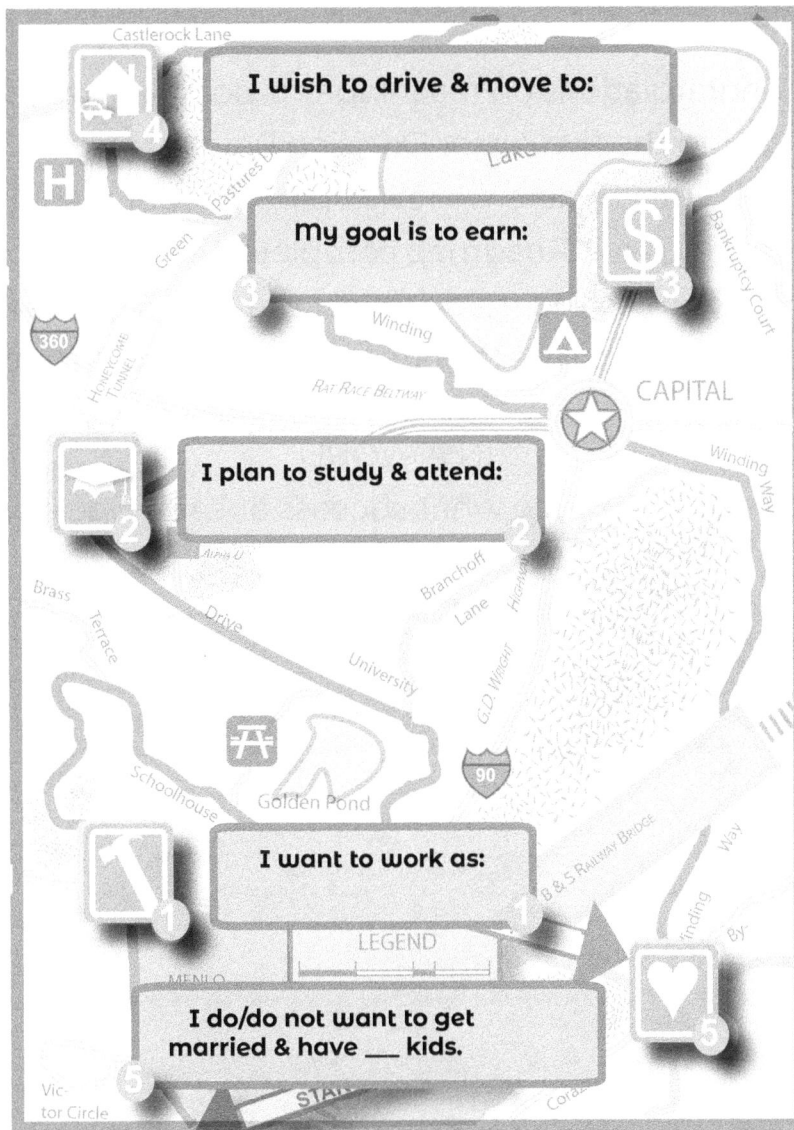

I wish to drive & move to:

My goal is to earn:

I plan to study & attend:

I want to work as:

I do/do not want to get married & have ___ kids.

LEGEND

If you don't know where you're going, then any road will take you there.

Lewis Carroll
(author, *Alice's Adventures in Wonderland*)

All righty then! Congratulations on reaching this point in the workbook after successfully navigating the five major Decision Points. Now, we are going to shift into Overdrive! Here is where we revisit parts of your planning process that will assist you in making your Roadmap complete. Reflect on your decision-making to see if the choices you made reflect the person you are or want to be. This is also an opportunity to reflect upon what "drove you" to your decisions.

IN A WORD

Using only one (1) word, describe what success at each Decision Point would mean to you:

Using only one (1) sentence, answer each of the following questions; make your answers as simple and direct as possible so that a third grader could understand or so that you could tell someone on an elevator without having to follow up with more sentences to explain what you just said:

1. What is it that you are most proficient at and passionate about?

2. For how long do you plan to go to school after high school?

3. How much money will you be earning ten years from now?

4. In ten years, what will you be driving and where will you live?

5. Will you get married and/or have kids?

The one thing I didn't really think about before I read Chapter 1 was:

> **a**

The one thing I would like to learn more about after reading Chapter 1 is:

> **b**

The most challenging exercise from Chapter 1 was:

> **c**

Rearview Review

CHAPTER  CAREER

 Out of 100 Career choices, the one I am most interested in is:

fill with choice from page 8, or insert your own

 I will sell my time/knowledge to the market doing the following:

based upon question on page 10, how would you like to get paid?

 For training purposes, I plan to gain experience in exchange for a fixed salary for my first Career so that I can ultimately do what I really want for my second Career. If I had to make a decision today, based upon my answers in this chapter, I would start off doing:

fill in first Career in the box above, fill in second Career in the box below

I have successfully reached my 1st Decision Point!

I want to work as:

2

The one thing I didn't really think about before I read Chapter 2 was:

> **a**

The one thing I would like to learn more about after reading Chapter 2 is:

> **b**

The most challenging exercise from Chapter 2 was:

> **c**

Rearview Review

CHAPTER ② EDUCATION

1 Out of 5 college majors closely aligned to topics I like, the one I am most interested in is:

fill with choice from page 30, or insert your own

3 After completing the college chart, ranking what is important to me in the Brain Storm and seeing how I feel about the distance of the school from home, the top three schools that best fit my needs are:

complete based upon answers from pages 34-37

5 If I had to make a decision today, all other things being equal with respect to financial aid and my academic portfolio, I would attend:

fill with preferred choice from above answer box

I have successfully reached my 2nd Decision Point!

I plan to study and attend:

The one thing I didn't really think about before I read Chapter 3 was:

The one thing I would like to learn more about after reading Chapter 3 is:

The most challenging exercise from Chapter 3 was:

Rearview Review

CHAPTER 3 CAPITAL

In order to accumulate Capital, the percentage or amount I wish to save/invest monthly is:

fill based upon answers from page 49

After completing the Lottery Win Wish List, I see that there are various Possessions that I would like to acquire. In the event I do not win the lottery, I would need this much Capital to acquire everything on my list:

list the total from the items listed on page 51

If I had to make a decision today, in light of how long it will take me to possibly earn $1M, I would like to start earning this amount annually:

based upon Career choice from Chapter 1, state desired reasonable salary

I have successfully reached my 3rd Decision Point!

My goal is to earn:

The one thing I didn't really think about before I read Chapter 4 was:

a

The one thing I would like to learn more about after reading Chapter 4 is:

b

The most challenging exercise from Chapter 4 was:

c

Rearview Review

CHAPTER  POSSESSIONS

 After evaluating all of the associated expenses with a vehicle, I am looking to spend this amount monthly:

state amount willing to pay monthly for car note from page 63

 After analyzing the "other" expenses necessary for home ownership, after moving out from my folks, I am most interested in moving to:

review expenses on pages 66-67 and think about where you would like to live

 If I had to make a decision today, all other things being equal, based upon my Career choice and expected Capital income, I am looking to buy or save up a down payment for a house that costs:

In light of the Advanced activity on page 64, insert a reasonable price

I have successfully reached my 4th Decision Point!

I wish to drive & move to:

The one thing I didn't really think about before I read Chapter 5 was:

The one thing I would like to learn more about after reading Chapter 5 is:

The most challenging exercise from Chapter 5 was:

Rearview Review

CHAPTER ⬦5⬦ COMPANIONSHIP

Based upon the information in this chapter, it merely confirms my opinion that with respect to getting married, I will:

fill with current preference

Based upon the information in this chapter, it merely confirms my opinion that with respect to having kids, I will:

fill with current preference

After completing the contents of this entire workbook, based upon the direction of my desired Roadmap and my timetable for doing so, when it comes to marriage and having kids, I will:

if you answered "Yes" for either of the above two, enter preferred timeframe

I have successfully reached my 5th Decision Point!

My preferred status is:

Don't forget to ASK YOUR FOLKS! While it may certainly appear that your folks or other important adults in your life have no earthly idea of what takes place within modern civilization, they come from an age not too far removed from the present, as primitive as they may seem at times. Our last piece of advice is to challenge yourself to question the living daylights out of them, and extract as much information from them as you can. They are repositories of your living history and will help you understand "this thing called life" as well as the life that you have lived thus far...

After completing this manual, I want to ask my folks more about:

1.

2.

3.

4.

5.

OK! Enough theory, time to practice. We now conclude so that you may begin. Wait a minute . . . do you hear that? The clock is ticking! The Time of Your Life awaits you!

Ready?

Get set . . .

Now GO!

THE GOODING TEAM

Sharon Gooding is a special education attorney who received her Master's degree in Education with an emphasis on at-risk youth. A former middle school teacher, Sharon is a life-long community advocate, having worked with a myriad of non-profit organizations dedicated to child development, and presently serves as an official Court Appointed Special Advocate. Sharon also consults with parents about how to better navigate the school system and advocate for the needs of one's child.

Frederick Gooding is an Associate Professor in *Texas Christian University's* Honors College who continues to travel the world in pursuit of his independent investigation of the truth.

FOR MORE INFORMATION

www.itslifetime.com

www.ingramcontent.com/pod-product-compliance
Lightning Source LLC
LaVergne TN
LVHW061301060426
835509LV00016B/1666